SLOUCHING
IN THE
UNDERGROWTH

For my sons

SLOUCHING
IN THE
UNDERGROWTH

THE LONG LIFE OF A GUNNER OFFICER

JACK SWAAB

FONTHILL

By the same author: *Field of Fire* (Alan Sutton, 2005)

Fonthill Media Limited
www.fonthillmedia.com
office@fonthillmedia.com

This edition published in the United Kingdom 2012

British Library Cataloguing in Publication Data:
A catalogue record for this book is available from the British Library

ISBN 978-1-78155-009-0 (print)
ISBN 978-1-78155-144-8 (e-book)

Typeset in 10pt on 14 pt Sabon LT.
Printed and bound in England.

Connect with us
 facebook.com/fonthillmedia twitter.com/fonthillmedia

Acknowledgements

I am very grateful to friends and family members who have provided me with photographs and memories which had slipped through my net; in particular, to Ken Dorrell and John Petty for recollections of a significant period of my advertising life. I am greatly indebted to my sons, Richard and Peter who have been generous with suggested revisions and corrections which have, I believe, fundamentally improved the end product.

What a big thank you I owe to Camilla Hill, who has transcribed every handwritten word onto her computer, and inserted, adjusted and emailed for months past.

And, finally, I want to thank Alan Sutton, publisher of this book as he was of my first, seven years ago.

CHAPTER 1

A LONDON CHILDHOOD
IN THE 1920s

I think that I knew it was cancer; but when the doctor said so, it still came as a shock. However, this isn't about my not-too-serious cancer surgery except as its function in kick-starting me into writing about my rather odd life. Odd? Well, yes, if you accept the dictionary definitions: unusual, peculiar in character, out of the way.

I was brought up rigidly British in the twenties by originally Dutch parents. Sent down from Oxford. Fleet Street reporter. Nearly seven years soldiering in desert, mud and snow. Post-war, found a wonderful wife, and less wonderful, a TB sanatorium. Cured and hectically successful in the merry-go-round of the international advertising world. Crashed and burned. Rose from the ashes into old age: hardly predictable after unwelcome health problems.

But, to go back to the beginning: my father was called Samuel Siegfried – always shortened to Sieg (with a soft, catarrhal g). My mother was Rachel Mina Henriette Van Straaten and always called Tel. In recent years my cousin Paul and others have traced our family back to 1725 on my mother's side, but had no success on my father's. He seems to have descended from poor peat farmers in Holland. Apparently working class, he went to South Africa aged fifteen to work on the railways. He told me he lived in Pretoria and used to see 'Lord Bobs' (Roberts) ride down the street on a white horse. Expelled by the British in the Boer war, he married my mother and they came to England and were naturalised as British citizens around the turn of the twentieth century. He worked for a Geneva-based company called Cargo Superintendents and was their Managing Director until he died aged sixty-six in 1946. Humble origins or not, he was fluent in French, German and English as well as his native Dutch. My mother was probably more middle class. She told me she was one of the first young ladies to ride her bicycle to work in Rotterdam. Ma died in 1964. She was eighty. Both my parents

Rachel Swaab aged about 34.

– particularly Dad – were voracious readers and played a mean hand of bridge. Dad was such an aggressive and critical partner that I was amazed that anyone would play with him. But he was very successful and there were two or three tables at home on many evenings.

As it was, I was brought up in a totally secular British household, sent to Sunday school – the Crusaders (!) – baptised and confirmed at my public school, only partly aware of my origins, and by now, more or less atheist by conviction. I remember when I was grown up, my mother telling me I couldn't be Jewish (I must have asked her about it) because I hadn't been circumcised! (Another of my mature experiences, by the way).

Meanwhile, I was to discover when my father died soon after the war that he'd secretly paid over the years for Jewish funeral rites and a plot in the cemetery at Willesden. Poor Pa. I did feel I must have been a disappointment to him. Sent down from Oxford. Deciding on journalism instead of something respectable. Redeemed, in some measure later, by my medal ribbons. Perhaps because I was his first born son, Dad was always a bit indulgent to me. To my elder sisters, he'd always been rather a tyrant. They used to call him 'Mr Barrett' after the play, *The Barretts of Wimpole Street*. He was a small man and they are sometimes apt to have a Napoleonic complex. As I said, he never tried to bully me.

The author's parents on their wedding day.

My early life was spent in a large, detached house called Andros in Sydenham, an undistinguished suburb in southeast London. My parents had earlier left a smaller nearby house during the Zeppelin air raids in 1917. A third daughter – Peggy – had been born in 1916 but died, along with many other children, when the milk had become infected. Many years later, rummaging in one of our huge wardrobes, I found a small white shoe. My mother had labelled it, 'a shoe from my baby's grave'. I wish now, that I'd asked where that grave was, but the matter was never discussed. Anyway, they'd moved to Bognor (not Regis then) where I was born on the rather ominous Ides of March in 1918 in a house called The Dugout. I spent some enjoyable summer holidays in Bognor as a small boy.

Back to Sydenham then. We had a cook called Lizzie and a nurse/housemaid I called Nag (originally Jessie Connor, doomed early to spinsterhood). Lizzie was a limited cook. I particularly hated – and refused to eat – her chocolate blancmange. The skin was so thick a mouse could have walked on it. My sisters used to call her lemon meringue, 'Vaseline on flannel'. Poor Lizzie was killed when her air raid shelter got a direct hit during a bombing raid. My potty training involved a rather unusual receptacle we called The Welsh Hat. I still remember sitting on it calling out 'I've d-a-a-a-n it', when Nag would come and wipe my bottom. When I didn't or couldn't 'do it' my mother resorted to the dreaded enema. It hung in the bathroom, evilly striped in red and black. I feared and hated what I called 'the gurgle, gurgle, spoot, spoot' (even this early having something of a talent for descriptive names). It probably accounts for my obsessively punctual bowel movements in later life.

The two elder sisters I mentioned earlier: Elly (ten years) and Bé (Louise actually but Bé to all, all her life) seven years older. They played naughty games with me, such as waking me and standing me up on the bed until I fell over. On the bus they'd call me 'Bertie' and pretended that I was mentally defective. They used to read me a favourite book which started, 'it was eight o'clock and long after Bertie's bed time ....'.

My sisters invented a language, presumably designed to enable them to speak privately. This was Urragoo – a word inserted with sentences: e.g. why would be wurragy, not norragot and so on. This sounds simple, but spoken at high speed – sometimes including French and Dutch words – it became almost unintelligible – and very secure for the users. I did speak Urragoo but not well. My own Swaabese is more difficult to learn, being totally irregular and without rules, and related to Newspeak (from George Orwell's *1984*).

Right at the top of Andros was a skylight above the landing and the attic. Bé used to make a weird face and as though flying called out in a ghostly

Elly, Dick, Jack and Bé,
c. 1929.

voice, 'the sky-y-y-ywaymen will get you'. I didn't know who they were - but
fled in terror. When I grew up, I used to call them Goneril (Elly) and Regan
(Bé) after King Lear's wicked daughters. But they loved me really and Bé who
was rather artistic, always made me a cut out cardboard London bus for my
Christmas stocking. Elly, a talented pianist, used to sing for me, 'Orpheus
with his lute made trees...', which always puzzled me until I discovered the
next line, 'and the mountain tops which freeze, bow themselves when he
did sing'. But my favourite was when Elly sang the aria *One Fine Day* from
Madame Butterfly. It has stayed with me all my life – 'then the trim white
vessel gli-i-des into the harbour' – as have my mother's piano pieces ... the
Liebestraum, some Chopin – her favourite, which I can still hum:

> Dum Dee Dee Dee Diddle Diddle Dum Dee Dee
> Diddle Dee Dum Dum Dum Dee Dee
> Dee Diddle Diddle Dum Dee Dee....

and later in life (through Zena) Mendelssohn's violin concerto, and some
Brahms and Bach and Tchaikovsky's Symphonie Pathétique. My mother
also played and sang. A bit of a control freak, she throbbed unconvincingly,
'Less than the dust beneath thy chariot wheels ... even less am I', and other
Indian love lyrics by Amy Woodforde-Finden.

Bé and daughters Ann Louise, Robbie and Monica, 1941.

Sometimes on Sunday mornings, my father would join in with his favourite: 'Come into the garden Maud, for the black bat night has flown ... I am here at the gate alo-oh-one'. Then he'd open the gin and angostura bitters (I was allowed a small glass of Avocaat). Quite often, on Sunday morning, the Antonious who lived nearby were asked for drinks in the drawing room. Mr A, an accountant at Dad's office, a dear little modest Greek, was desperately bullied by his large strident North Country wife and by the apple of their eye – 'Gracie', an extremely pretty but vapid blonde who in her teens decided to be called Pat. Unfortunate, henpecked Mr A – 'Spiro' – finally fled to the lavatory one day and enacted his ultimate act of rebellion – death on the seat.

My sisters used to have a dance – usually I think, at their eighteenth birthday. At Bé's eighteenth, I, not quite eleven, was lurking at the edge of the dance floor surreptitiously eyeing the local talent, when a friend of my sisters – Olga – oozed up to me crying out, 'come on, dance with me!' It was a Viennese waltz, something I only had vague recall of as 'one two three one two three'. With this I was clasped to Olga's generous bosom and engaged in a kind of swooning nightmare, rarely it seemed, touching the floor. My sisters had tried to make a dancer out of me, without much success; but I

Dick, Jack, and watering-can in the garden
at Andros.

remember late one wartime night when enhanced by drink I whirled an ex-
girlfriend called Griselda around the floor of the Dorchester (or was it the
Gro Ho?) in a dramatic rendering of the Tango.

My sisters duly got married; Elly to a plump, prosperous, Jewish New
Yorker she'd met on holiday in Madeira. At the Reception, Bé recited a poem
she'd written: 'A tale of romance I shall tell / How Elly met at Reid's Hotel
...'. They sent us generous food parcels and cigarettes in the war. After the
war, Elly courageously survived breast cancer. Her (much older) husband
died about then. Bé also met her husband, a Lancastrian, RC economist/
financial adviser on holiday in the Isle of Wight. He – also much older – lost
an eye in a bombing raid in the war. Bé had five daughters. One – shades of
her mother – died prematurely. One arrived late in life and (probably feeling
it to be an unlikely miracle) caused her to become a Roman Catholic ('It's
her age my dear', Elly explained to me). I think all that side of the family
lapsed.

Completing my siblings was Dick – born in 1921. He was usually called
Dickie. An early exploit involved the disappearance of some butter balls at
the tea table. 'Who ate the butter balls?' came the enquiry. The latest born
tot piped up 'Dittie' – as close as he could get. Dick was undoubtedly my

Gibraltar, 1942. On the far right of the front row Vivien Leigh and Dick Swaab.

mother's favourite. He was always plump and cheerful (I was thin – 'wiry' they said – and gloomy) but notoriously 'bilious', and tended to leave the table at meals to be sick – or just to feel sick. And sick he always was when we went abroad before the ship even left the dock. In 1942, my ship called at Gibraltar *en route* for the Middle East. Dick was a gunner there and we were able to have a drink together – but not, would you believe, at one of the officers' watering holes because he was another rank. So I drank with the ORs. I have a picture of Dick and his mates, stripped to the waist with an Ensa party. He's sitting next to Vivien Leigh, lucky fellow. Dick survived the war, only to be killed by a speeding motorist on New Year's Eve 1947. But more on that later.

Looking back, there were such good things in my early years ... the big bag of special fruit that Dad used to bring home after work on Saturday – peaches, melons, cherries, pineapple. And the Droste chocolates from Holland; all those exciting varieties layered in their little wooden boxes. Then there were the giant chocolate initials which we all received at birthdays and Christmas. Christmas .... sometimes blighted by a scene at dinner when Dad, who was possibly the world's worst carver, always used to rant about the bluntness of the carving knife as he set about wrecking the enormous turkey. One particularly bad year, Ma stormed from the table in tears. We all sat chewing in miserable silence as our Christmas dinner turned to sawdust.

At Christmas we children were blindfolded and had to wait in the hall as our parents and the maids unwrapped all the presents in the morning room. They were all laid out so we missed the thrill of unpacking them ourselves.

Once ready we were led into the morning room where the open fire blazed cheerfully. The strains of *Oh Come All Ye Faithful* rang out from the wind-up gramophone. The scales were then as it were removed from our eyes and we beheld all the presents under and around the big, glistening tree with its lighted candles (which often caught fire – another minor crisis!) and plentiful chocolate ornaments. Christmas for my own family wasn't so very different except that we all unwrapped our presents in turn, one at a time, wallowing in paper chaos. Also, the tree lights by then were electric; but the chocolate ornaments were equally omnipresent. Also, *I* was a good carver – though the family hated my electric knife.

On Christmas afternoons, soggy with food, we lay around eating crystallised fruits – always sent by one of Dad's business friends – and chocolate ornaments from the tree, as we read our Christmas present books. I always had the new *William*. There must have been a dozen on my bookshelf ..... *Just William, More William, William the Outlaw*, on they went. Thinking back, it seems that the only person who didn't get much in the way of presents was Dad. Not that finding something was easy, as all his suits were virtually identical save for minor colour differences; and starched collars, shirts, anonymous ties, etc, ditto. My mother, when asked, used to say, 'he'd like some socks' (which she bought) so he was never short of those. Dad's wardrobe varied slightly in summer. At the beach it would be a soft collar, no spats or boots, but more casual shoes and no homburg. I have a photograph of him on the beach (at Bognor probably) flying my box kite. He holds the string skywards while I stand behind him (in school cap, blazer and shorts) holding the spool. Dad is wearing a flat cap and white shoes and seems to be smoking a cigar.

Actually, he didn't spend much time at the seaside but stayed in town, possibly getting up to naughtiness. We occasionally had a lady visitor called Annie. The girls called her 'Dick's mother' but nobody ever verified that claim. Another protégée (years later) was Vera (who occupied my bedroom). Dad took her to sing for Elisabeth Schumann whom he evidently knew. She got the thumbs down and there was a stormy scene at home that evening.

Dressed for the beach, flying a kite in Bognor.

I know that one tends to glorify the past, but we had wonderful holidays. Apart from Bognor, we had a hired house in Westcliff and later used to stay at The Savoy Hotel (not quite the best one) in Sandown on the Isle of Wight. A chap there had a game which involved trapping ping pong balls in water which swirled round a large circular holder. He used to summon trade by crying out, 'The more players the bigger the prize!' (which was always chocolate bars of different sizes). He'd crank the handle and the ping pong balls flew round in the water. 'Hit the little devils on the head, they must go in!' he'd call out. We would then plunge the little pots with one way metal bars into the water. I realised early that the secret was to drop in really gently. Thus I accumulated several dozen chocolate bars until he finally banned me from playing. It was my first major sporting success. I have to admit that these have not been numerous. I was captain of swimming at my prep school (about which, more later) but far outclassed by my son Richard who swims vast distances every year. Later, I was a fairly good slip fielder and rather limited opening batsman; put to shame by my son Peter with his four or five thousand runs topping the list at his club. However, I *was* captain of shooting – something the boys happily had no chance of emulating.

Dick, Jack, Elly and Bé at Bognor,
c. 1923.

By today's standards, I was allowed amazing freedom at the seaside. I'd wander round for hours occasionally joining in some beach cricket game or swimming. Elly had taught me to swim early in life and I soon outstripped the girls. Ma couldn't swim and always backed into the sea exclaiming, 'Oof, oof!'. Dad never entered the sea in his life. The nearest he came was one year when I fired a sort of airplane from my catapult. It descended from the sky and landed just above his eye as he sat reading the paper in his deckchair. He pursued me, roaring with rage, but I fled far into the sea until, dancing furiously at the verge, he gave up the pursuit. I stayed away until evening.

I can still bring to mind the damp, briny smell of the beach hut we used to hire. There were sandwiches, ice cream and various goodies there throughout the day. Seems it was never raining. Later in life I came across Tennyson's The Lotos-Eaters where, 'In the afternoon they came unto a land / In which it seemèd always afternoon', and it put me in mind of those apparently idyllic summer holidays.

We also holidayed in Holland. Days started with the exciting hired Daimlers which lurched, loaded with our enormous trunks, to Liverpool Street. Thence on steam trains to Harwich and the sea journey to the Hook

Jack and Dick with their father and aunts in Holland, c. 1928.

of Holland. There, I first encountered the fat little aunties and uncles, all later to end their days choking on Zyklon B gas. We didn't swim in Holland (at Scheveningen, Noordwijk and Bergen opzee) but I have a picture of Dick and me with Dad and two aunts (one, I think, was Tante Céline) in the large straw chairs like upturned shoes. Dad holds me, suited and embarrassed, and Dick scowls from an aunt's lap.

My parents never overtly discussed our Jewish background. I think that they may have feared latent anti-Semitism. Thus it was not until I entered my teens that – however reluctantly – I had to acknowledge my ancestry with its inevitable implications and encounters. But I was always grateful to them for coming to England some hundred years ago, and sparing me – unlike almost the entire Dutch family – death in Auschwitz, Treblinka, Sobibor and the rest.

I must tell you about Forest Hill House School (motto *Certum Pete Finem* – take straight aim). In *Decline and Fall*, Evelyn Waugh describes the prep school Llanabba which, bizarre though it was, did not outshine FHHS to which, aged seven, I was sent as a weekly boarder. The Headmaster, A. Y. Watson-Miller, was an almost legendary figure (being rarely seen with his shadowy wife.) His young daughter, Margaret however, used to display her unique reproductive charms to privileged students in the bike shed. Then there were the brothers Gray; rather like Jacob and Esau – one smooth and sinister, the other large with a huge shock of unruly hair.

At the end of the academic year, the school gave a sort of concert at which the larger Gray intoned a poem about Laska – who apparently suffered a violent death. I can still hear him: 'Was that thunder? No, by the Lord. It was only the trampling of the herd!' he would bellow. And finally, in a broken voice: 'Laska .... lay *dead*'.

My contribution, or at least the one I recall, was a recitation from *The Ancient Mariner*. Bent double and false-bearded I recited many stanzas in what I took to be a quavering old man's voice: 'All in a hot and copper sky, The bloody (bloody!) Sun, at noon, Right up above the mast did stand, No bigger than the Moon'. Pointing skywards, I particularly enjoyed the delicious naughty word so lawfully intoned!

There was a rich mixture of pupils aged up to at least deep teenage. I remember Badini from Italy who tried to seduce me. He would sneak into my bed and fondle my tiny penis; I, totally unresponsive, was deeply embarrassed. Danish Bock tried the reverse – with similar lack of success. Then we had Zafar Ali and Zakok Ali from, I think, Egypt; Mr Miller's nephew, Burleigh, a handsome bully, somebody – name forgotten – from Omaha, Nebraska and Danischewsky, who I believe went on to do well in the film industry. Nor must I omit Tony Crump and Crapper my main rivals in spelling, and the weekly form order, for which a cup was awarded each year. (I usually won it, displaying it in a cabinet in the drawing room.) Actually, I was reasonably well educated at this funny little school and I have found two yellowing Certificate of Honour documents headed with the school crest and motto, awarded 'for being first in more than two Form subjects'. In 1928, I was apparently first in seven, and in 1929 no less than nine.

Mr Vredenburg a rather handsome Nordic type didn't reappear one term, disappearing at the same time as a very pretty boy called Denis Ryall. We knew that something untoward was behind this, but were too innocent (unlike today's children) to know exactly what. By the same token, there was a terrible row one year because someone had apparently said that Mr Lewis (another master) and Miss Bartlett (a rather hunchbacked small teacher) had 'become engaged'. Why this was such a heinous crime was never made clear but we all had to stand trembling before The Deity Miller and apologise. We all did, without having any idea why. I became a very good swimmer at this school. We used to go to the local baths once or twice a week and afterwards, to the baker's shop to enjoy warm fresh penny buns.

The football second XI. The author is second from the right in the front row.

I also played soccer. I have a photograph of the second eleven. There I sit, the second smallest boy, arms folded, in my white sweater; for in spite of my lack of inches, I was apparently the goalkeeper. At the end of the row, pretty little Denis Ryall. At each end stands a Mr Gray in gown and plus fours. Next to me, the captain, a large boy holding the ball inscribed '2nd XI, 1929-30'. So I was about twelve and in my last year before public school. I learned to bat at cricket – taught one-to-one by the reprehensible Mr Vredenburg who, happily, had no designs on me other than to ensure that I played a straight bat.

The Matron was little, elderly (as it seemed) Mrs Long. Later in life, I wondered about her origins because if you did something she found unacceptable, she would call you a Stupid Head. So I presume that she had some kind of Teutonic wartime connection, this still being the twenties. I have to say that in spite of all the oddities, I was well taught. In class, if we wished to be excused we had to ask in French, and we had intensive spelling tests every week, for which less than 19 out of 20 was regarded (by me and aforementioned rivals) as failure. We sang *Drink to Me Only*, *Frère Jacques* and *Sur le Pont d'Avignon* and *D'ye Ken John Peel?* and each day's assembly began with the Lord's Prayer which I thought started 'Our Father which charted Heaven', which made perfectly good sense to me then (not sure it still doesn't).

Above all, I acquired a love of poetry and Shakespeare in particular, so that aged thirteen I passed in five subjects and with flying colours The Oxford University Junior Local Examination. (The set play was *Julius Caesar* and I sometimes wonder what the examiner made of my answer to 'your favourite character' – Cassius).

At the end of each year, we had a dormitory feast late at night. This consisted of crisps, Scotch eggs, ginger beer and similar treats. It was on these occasions that the lustful seniors initiated their shameful designs on my person.

It is difficult to believe in these days of Health and Safety but when the weather froze, we poured water all the way down the playground (which sloped) and formed an ice slide down which we hurled ourselves at maximum speed. Many were the bruises and skinned knees on which iodine was poured – by the unsympathetic Mrs Long. In the Easter term, the Boat Race was an obsessive topic. Not that going to Oxford or Cambridge was in anyone's thoughts, even if I did a decade later, but we all sported a favour; light or dark blue and were intensely partisan. Health and Safety would also have disapproved of our unswerving devotion to conker fighting. I remember how the apparently strong new shiny conkers were quickly demolished by the veteran seventy-eighters, the higher the number the more victories that gnarled red conker would have won. A bit like Matthew Arnold's Sohrab and Rustum where the fresh young hero is killed by his unknowing father. I still read this poem at regular intervals, and – softy that I am – always end up with tears in my eyes. 'Welling' they call that in the soap operas I now watch. Conkers achieved reputation and seniority by acquiring the victories of defeated rivals. Thus a nineteener which defeated a fourteener became a 'thirty three-er' and spectacular was the clash of two fifty plus gnarled veterans.

Going to the flicks was a major treat in my young school days. There were several cinemas in Sydenham and Forest Hill: The State in Sydenham Road (now a Tesco) and The Rink, while in Forest Hill we had The Capitol. Each had coloured wall panels which lit up during the organ display on the mighty Wurlitzer which rose up in spot-lit splendour from the depths in front of the screen. Usually the organ display was accompanied by slides or film. I remember *Finlandia* accompanied by the snow-clad Finnish landscape. There was also a little fleapit in Sydenham Road called (I think) The Classic. They showed 'nature' films which gave us our first view of naked breasts. But as they were flourished by black ('nature') girls, the films weren't classified as A – which necessitated being taken inside by a friendly, acquiescent adult. The excitement of those splendid, forbidden fruits!

Sydenham Road now so identikit ... I remember Mr Macrae the chemist (where I sometimes helped in the holidays) and the greengrocer where we bought strawberries in brown paper bags. There was Williamson the grocer's at Cobbs Corner where I bought provisions each term for my tuckbox (made by me at carpentry class; very inexpertly). How different was Sainsbury's with its long marble counter behind which large men in aprons wielded noisy wooden clappers, transforming huge blocks of butter into a 'pound of best fresh' in seconds. And their porky sausages which I used for my Scouts' cooking badge. Cooked on a fire skilfully built and lit with one match only.

We were influenced by the films. In particular it must have been the 1925 *Ben-Hur* which gave rise to a particular activity at Forest Hill House. We were charioteers. Two boys, usually agile and/or speedy, linked arms behind their backs. They were the horses. A third, larger boy 'drove' them at other chariots with the aim of knocking one to the ground. My companion horse was a very nice boy called Butterfield. Our driver was the enterprising lascivious Dane, Bock. I seem to remember that we were champions, Bock being an imperious charioteer and Butterfield and I surprisingly courageous – at the cost of many a grazed knee when we fell at speed, as we pranced and snorted. Cecil B would have been proud of us.

And I remember the solemnity of Armistice Day so well. One year I was shopping at Cobb's Corner in Sydenham, Cobb's being our only department store. That morning the buses all stopped (numbers 2, 3, 12, 49) and stood in silence. We heard the guns boom far away to end the two minutes, during which nobody spoke or moved. I pay an occasional visit to Sydenham and Cobb's Corner from time to time. The shops have changed. No more State cinema nor the man with 'Mutt and Jeff', the general service war medals, who sat on the bridge selling matches. Shamefully I used to avert my eyes.

I used to know those old buses almost as family: the way the driver of No 2 used to reach gratingly for the gear as we gasped our way up to Crystal Palace where there was a sort of terminus, including, I think No 3 and No 49a. There was the 75 which you caught at the bottom of Mayow Road. It went to Penge where trains to Victoria ran every 15 minutes. Trains from Sydenham went to London Bridge. And I think it was 49a which Dad and I used to take for an occasional outing to Tooting Bec Common. (It was on one of these Sunday outings that he – possibly instructed by Ma – embarked on what I presume was to be 'the facts of life' as I was soon to go off to boarding school. He had just started on, 'There may be other boys who ...' when, deeply embarrassed I blurted out, 'Oh yes, I know all about that' (not that I did). 'Oh well, that's all right then,' murmured my much relieved parent; and that was the sum total of my sex education. I remember the location: the top of Berryman's Lane just off Mayow Road.

But I was talking about buses. They were mostly General (LGOC) with the occasional Thomas Tilling – deeper red and with a different engine note. All open on top of course, where you sat on a slatted wooden seat. When it rained there was a hard tarpaulin you could pull up to cover most of your torso. Buses did have obligatory stops and request stops but quite often were obliging enough to stop anywhere if you held out a questing hand. There was always a conductor with tickets held by springs on a wooden container. The tickets were all different colours starting with the white, the cheapest – about ½p in today's money – to rather glamorous red or purple which might have cost 8 or 9 pence in old money. When you'd bought your ticket, the conductor inserted it into a metal gadget he hung round his neck and punched, with a ringing sound, a small hole against the stop at which you'd alighted. This was for the benefit of the occasional inspector who came round barking out 'tickets please'.

One day there were rumours of buses with enclosed upper decks and sure enough I saw one of these in Sydenham Road – the 108 which went to Bromley by Bow. It was said to be lower than the others so that it could get through the Blackwall Tunnel, but I never tested the accuracy of this, and indeed only ever took a 108 a few times as it didn't go where I wanted to go. However, I still recall my first closed upstairs trip. I was walking in Dartmouth Road near Forest Hill when, hearing a strange kind of whirring engine, I looked round to see a hitherto unknown Thomas Tilling (I think a 12a) approaching. Boldly I stuck out my hand. The driver – perhaps anxious to demonstrate his new charge – stopped; and I scampered up the steps, now all covered in, and up to the exciting weatherproof upper deck. Buses became more and more glamorous and comfortable, the six-wheeled LT for example and electric trolley buses, until today, when they are positively luxurious and, what a blessing to me, *free*.

I have been back to Andros occasionally with Zena and Richard and I've been reminded of a TV programme called *Bargain Hunt*. So many items auctioned there could have been mine for Andros was full of them ... the grandfather clock in the hall, the Tantalus in the morning room, a pantry full of Clarice Cliff and Susie Cooper chinaware which we used daily. Alas, after the war my mother cleared the house (which was given over to Belgian refugees in the war) while I was still away in the army. And with it all my treasured cigarette card collections, swopped and re-swopped till every card was new: Flags of the World, Railway Engines, Motor Cars, Cricketers, Footballers, Wild Flowers (in special albums) and more. Also to oblivion went my theatre programmes (there must have been over fifty), school magazines and other souvenirs. I never quite forgave Ma for that.

The first film I saw (at the Rink in Silverdale — long gone) was Buster Keaton in *The General*. Later – taken in by some kindly adult because there were unofficial solo age limits – I saw Bela Lugosi in *Dracula* which frightened me so much that for ages I wouldn't open my bedroom window at night, even in a hot summer. I remembered a scene in the film where an apparent bat had flown in the window and metamorphosed into the dreaded Count.

When I was rather older and home for the holidays a friend and I would visit three cinemas a day in the West End, starting with the New Victoria where the 10.30 seats were only 1/6d (7½p) and thence to the Carlton and the Ritz or the Rialto. By five o'clock we'd emerge copiously entertained and with shattering headaches. Again, as I grew older, my father used to take me – and sometimes Ma and the girls – to the theatre. We'd wear black tie and the ladies evening dress. In the Smith's Dataday which I kept for years and which has disappeared up to 1937, I see that in that year I saw ninety films, eighteen plays (and *La Bohème* in Genoa) and read eighty-two books. The films are categorised with one star for Praiseworthy up to four stars: A Great Film. Recipients of four stars include *All Quiet on the Western Front*, *Dead End* and *I am a Fugitive from the Chain Gang*. (Wasn't Paul Muni splendid?) I kept up this rather anally retentive habit until 1939 where the totals were: films 56, plays 9 and books 115.

I remember Dad took me to see Galsworthy's *Loyalties* – not that either of us alluded to the background – too emotive, with its wrongly despised Jew finally vindicated.

Dad was a bit of a tease. Sometimes when we were all in the dining room, he'd take a handful of change from his trouser pocket, and opening and enclosing his fist several times, would say 'Guess the amount and you can keep it'. Nobody ever did. One year he discovered the Fuller's chocolate Easter eggs which were real eggs emptied and filled with delicious cream enclosed by plain chocolate and hard as rocks. At breakfast, we all tapped in vain to eat our 'boiled eggs' until someone discovered the disguise. Nobody cared because the eggs were delicious and thereafter an annual favourite.

Pa was deeply idiosyncratic. We were only allowed white bread, perhaps because of the dark 'impure' shade of brown. He used to make us eat bread sandwiches, layers of bread on bread, at breakfast. Bé used to hide hers in her knickers and then on the top of one of the wardrobes: heaven for the mice which were always around; you'd hear them scratching about at night. Dad also *hated* an open door. I think like Emma's father, Mr Woodhouse, he feared the malign influence of draughts. 'Shut the door!' he'd bark (in Dutch). As I grew older and cheekier I'd say, 'Should I go out or through?'. He was a dedicated hypochondriac whose actual hobby later in life was visiting the doctor, who humoured him and did his own bank account no harm. Sadly – and not really realised – he did get angina. Told by a Harley Street specialist that he should go immediately to bed as things were serious, he did so; and died within weeks. I often felt he was literally scared to death. This was in May 1946 long before bypasses etc. I had just been demobbed and at the home of my (what else can I call her?) lover was summoned in the night by my mother wailing over the phone, 'He's *dying* ... come back'. I drove through the darkness in my unreliable car. Pa was indeed dying, as his intermittent chain-stokes breathing made clear, and lasted only a few hours. I remember how in death his face seemed to become quite youthful. I was immensely saddened and felt (as I have already said) that I didn't live up to his hopes or expectations. I did, later perhaps – but what use was that?

In today's paper, I was reading about a drug called Finasteride which they give (or, anyway, gave me) for a condition called bph-enlarged prostate. It seems that they now suspect that it can lead to some types of cancer. Just as one week red wine prevents a heart attack and the next it provokes one. My lifetime has been a saga of contradictory – even if well intentioned – medical lore.

Mind you, thinking back to some of my early medical memories, I'm surprised I was ever persuaded to enter a hospital; not that I had much choice. Aged five it was deemed necessary to remove my tonsils; Kings College Hospital was the venue. Terrified, I was led into the operating theatre – no pre-med or soothing talk in those days. Some grim white-clad creatures seized me, laid me protesting on the table, placed a sort of gas mantle over my face and proceeded to land drop after drop of ether upon it. It was utterly horrible to smell and I struggled in vain to escape. In due course I awoke in a huge room full of men – their ward, as there were no children's wards it seems. All I can remember is playing with a clockwork train on the floor. Next time I was seven. For years walking and exercise had given me a fierce pain in my side. They called it The Stitch. Anyway we were at Westcliff (the posh end of Southend) for a month in a hired house, and I had taken a long walk along the mud flats towards the sea at low tide.

When the tide turned it did so at a swift pace and driven by panic I ran for the shore. I ended up jack-knifed with The Stitch and that very evening saw me in a local nursing home being readied to have my appendix removed. This time, once more surrounded by alien monsters, I was held down and a sort of rubber mask put over my face. Once again that terrible smell, an increasingly loud buzzing; and oblivion. I have to admit that it got rid of The Stitch, but not my fear of anaesthetic ; reduced I must admit by more considerate modern methodology. But about Finasteride.

As it happens, after eleven years on Finasteride I ended up with a prostate operation called a turp. I had always thought that my penis was intended to be a one way passage; not a shortcut for a camera into my innards; an experience to be avoided. Oh the hours I could – but won't – spend describing the saga of desperate failure to urinate, the insertion (ouch) and removal (ouch) of catheters. My operation was performed by a dazzlingly attractive Indian lady. Seeing my ill-disguised surprise, she assured me, 'I'm very good'. She popped up between my dead legs (I had an epidural) with a cheery good morning and I never saw her again to thank her as I peed copiously at will. Some years later, I was to experience again the unwelcome questing camera. (Details later, perhaps).

CHAPTER 2

1930s. WEYMOUTH COLLEGE
AND OXFORD

Anyway my prostate was the last thing on my mind – in fact I didn't know it existed – when in September 1931, I went to boarding school at Weymouth College (*Perseverando Vincimus* –By persevering we conquer) in Dorset. I have to say that my first year there was exceedingly unhappy. Unlike boarding school today, Weymouth was nearer to Tom Brown's times. The food would now probably cause a riot at Wandsworth or Wormwood Scrubs. The dormitories with their Spartan iron bedsteads were unheated and had no running water. Under each bed an enamel chamber pot – called a Jerry. We young boys had to wear Eton collars for our first year, and there were stringent rules imposed by the seniors, governing the right to put one hand, later two, in your trouser pocket. Failure to observe these rules was regarded as 'side'. To be 'sidey' was a grave offence which warranted severe physical punishment. At that stage – pale, thin, four feet eleven with a funny name – I was 'a weed'. A weed was not a good thing to be and marked you out as prime bullying material.

As I lay, cold and homesick on my first morning, the dormitory door opened and there was a loud roar. 'Get down to ba-a-aths'. We huddled naked and (in my case) dreadfully embarrassed, before immersing ourselves in several baths of icy water. These were usually left full overnight and in the Easter term were frequently topped by a thin layer of ice. In another group of baths the other side of the house lay the lordly prefects, relaxing in the steaming hot water, possibly shaving in an indolent way which seemed to underline the difference between their lifestyle and ours. I discovered fairly soon that a cold bath was slightly less horrible if you could seize yourself to spend a little while in it. Ten seconds, say.

Early on, I was marked for persecution by an extremely unpleasant frog-faced person some years my senior. The first manifestation was when, playing rugger for the first time, he punched me on the nose. But much more was to come. Reporting of an afternoon to the empty dormitory, I had to strip, lie on the bed for inspection – but not handling – and finally get beaten – usually with a slipper. The reason, it was made clear to me, was that I was sidey. He, MA, had been deputed by a group to supervise my treatment, and it was made clear that any attempt to publicise my punishment would result in penalties too horrible to contemplate. I've not given this person's name because even now it fills me with revulsion. For some years, I scanned the obits in *The Daily Telegraph* and was able on a certain date to feel a measure of pleasure ... and what? Relief perhaps?

Something happened on the last night of my last term which has probably remained a secret until this very moment. A friend of mine, G. D. Templer (always called Larry), told me that he had abstracted from its packing case a much-cherished wireless belonging to Daddy Blake. In its place he had substituted several large German dictionaries. Of course, I never discovered how this played out; and we can't find out now because poor old Larry was killed by the Japanese while working on the infamous Death Railway in Burma.

The end of my ordeal with MA and his (almost certainly fictitious) group came about through my friendship (lifelong) with Roden Parry. (Parry III, Parry I being George, Parry II, Alan and – later – Parry IV, Peter). It so happened that George had noticed my slipper-created bruises at baths and asked Roden to investigate. Disregarding the fearful consequences of speaking out, I told all. Somebody spoke to MA and my time of trial ended abruptly.

Something, then, about the Parry family. The Revd – Roden's father – had been a Welsh rugby international winger. He was now Vicar of an East End parish. I used to stay there in the enormous vicarage in the holidays and read the lesson occasionally. As I said, I was baptised at Weymouth and Roden was one of my godfathers. The other was George Russ and we were known as The Old Firm. In my previous book *Field of Fire*, I relate how we all met in a Brussels hospital to which I had been sent when wounded in 1944. The Parrys all had a third initial M. (G. E. M., A. J. M., R. K. M., P. F. M.) which stood for Maule. I think this was Mrs Parry's family name (I don't think I ever knew what Mr and Mrs were called). She *was* vaguely aristocratic and always much involved with the Court section in *The Times* and *Daily Telegraph*. The Revd had a strange habit of inserting, 'I mean to say don't you know' into his conversation.

Alas, they are all dead now (why aren't I?). George was the army padre immortalised in the film *The Longest Day*. He elected to stay with the wounded during the early days in Normandy and was shot by the SS for his bravery. Alan was wounded but insisted on being wheel-chaired into battle. He, a regular soldier and always regarded as not too bright, received the Military Cross. Peter, the youngest, doted on by his mother, was killed in Tobruk in 1942. Roden became a Lt-Colonel and had a rather distinguished post war career. He and his wife Mary had a daughter, Libby. She sent me his funeral service as I couldn't get to Coombe Bissett where he finally lived. In her letter she wrote, 'Daddy often spoke of you with affection'. I miss him. And so many others.

The next five years at Weymouth probably turned me – for better or worse – into the person I was to become. But I do remember one thing (once again bowel-connected I'm afraid) from my first few weeks; the lavatories had no doors. No doubt this was intended as a deterrent to the ever-present obsession with sex. In one section was the House of Commons, where we lesser mortals had to exercise our normal – but definitely not abnormal – functions. In another, the House of Lords was where the prefects – also without doors – performed. As Lady Chatterley's gamekeeper pointed out to her, she too 'had to piss and shit' and I suppose, in addition to the veto on forbidden pleasures, it was felt to be a sort of anal democracy. Anyway, to one brought up in a household much given to privacy, the idea of public defecation was not to be contemplated. However, only lavatories with doors in the school were exclusively for the masters. After ten days or so of enforced constipation, I sneaked back from our Sunday afternoon walk and (painfully) resolved my problem. I think I fairly soon reconciled myself to the smelly House of Commons; and in due course had no problem with the House of Lords.

The lack of privacy already violated by morning baths was further augmented by lying, like sardines, half a dozen at a time in the shallow baths we used when 'muddied oafs at the goal'. Penile classifications were Cavaliers (uncircumcised) and Roundheads, who outnumbered them by about ten to one. I was a deceitful cavalier and remained one for another twenty years. When finally modified, it was for what you might call functional, and not religious or tribal reasons. (My mother once told me – I'm not sure how the question arose – that I couldn't be a Jew because I hadn't been circumcised.)

As I've said, I was a weed and as such remained fairly anonymous until my first summer term. Then, long-forgotten Mr Vredenburg's tuition enabled me to emerge as one who might in the distant future be some use at cricket. But it was another event which changed my lowly status to mild fame.

Each summer term, the Headmaster set a general knowledge exam which had to be taken by every pupil. The marks ran into nearly 200 and were scaled back to 100, and the results posted on the main notice-board. To the astonishment of all, there at number two was this weed, Swaab. This earned me grudging respect and I became, as it were, a real person. (To boast: in my last year I came first with a record gap to the runner-up).

I ought to record some of the Staff *Dramatis Personae*. The Headmaster was a large, awe-inspiring man who had won a Military Cross at Kut el Amara in 1917. His nickname was Pogger or Poggy. When administering a beating which I experienced only once, he used a large cudgel and a fearful vein appeared on his forehead. I think this possibly presaged his early death, when, after appointment to a much more illustrious school, he suddenly fell dead at a public dinner. I had the privilege in my last year of one-to-one English tuition. Specifically we undertook a deep analysis of Tennyson's *In Memoriam*.

The second master was H. W. Major always known as Gobi because he was fat. (The Gobi Desert is described as a Great Waste.) Gobi died of pneumonia a year or two into my stay, and was much mourned.

Then there was E. J. (Eileen) Roberts, universally known as The Hag. Never called anything else. She had come as a replacement during the War and had stayed ever since. She instituted the Library Essay Prize which I won in 1936. The Hag had a broad Scottish accent, and I so well recall how when we mucked about doing crowd scenes in a *Julius Caesar* reading she would single out some rowdy ringleader with the cry, 'It's people like you that *spoil* it all!'

Next The Priest, Housemaster of college house and also an MC – won at Passchendaele. He used to say of that fearful killing ground, 'we had to rear in our helmets'. The Priest was a great photographer and used to take us on expeditions to the many churches in Dorset. I became mildly knowledgeable about Gothic and perpendicular architecture and other clerical aspects. The desirable thing on Sundays – which were a dead zone – was to be asked to tea with The Priest. There was cake and a gramophone and the repertoire always included *Eleven More Months & Ten More Days* and *Abdul the Bulbul Emir*. I wasn't one of the Priest's favourites (doubts always persisted regarding his inclinations) so I didn't get to Sunday tea very often. Mr Hamilton was an inebriated Irishman who taught (or, in my case, singularly failed to teach) physics. His favourite punishment was, 'a half swing with the metre rule' – quite painful. One day we each wrote one letter H.A.M.B.O.N.E on the blackboard before he came in. On his demanding the culprit we all stood up; and to each was a full swing of the meter rule administered.

Colvin-Smith, the English teacher had been an actor somewhere, sometime. His lessons were always dramatic, and deepened and enlarged my growing love of Shakespeare. I owe 'Colvine' which we called him, a great deal.

I can't say the same of F. Bush, the mathematics man, always known as 'Sam' Bush. He failed to turn me into a good mathematician because I found maths boring and incomprehensible. To this day, I can't work out what a quadratic equation was *for*. By some miracle, I managed a credit in school certificate, one of six which automatically gave me Matric and thus no need to sit Responsions, the Oxford University entrance exam.

J. J. G. Walkington (Captain and CO of the school OTC) was always known as 'Tor'. Tor's lessons (French? not sure) tended to be boring. When asking a boy a question he had a habit, if the boy didn't seem to know the answer, of querying, 'surely?' or sometimes 'surely surely?' To add interest, I used to have a sweepstake on how many 'surelys' there would be in a given lesson. He didn't seem to notice the occasional excited exclamation as one of us reached the selected target. And yes, I got a French credit too. I can still forge his signature – and indeed E. V. T. The Priest and A. G. Pite, Headmaster. These initials featured in the *Daily Report*. The *Daily Report* was designed mainly for boys who were a bit stupid or those who either through laziness or indifference were getting bad results in form work. These misfits had a notebook in which was entered every lesson and the teacher's verdict on their performance. When, stung by the stigma of *DR*, I collected 'Excellent' or 'Very Good' for virtually every lesson, I was taken off after one term and told by the Headmaster to stop being so silly! Great man.

There were other masters: Stewart-Clark with the pretty wife, J. W. S. 'Daddy' Blake with the Rover which had the freewheel and T. S. Nevill who became Headmaster after Pite left. He didn't like me and although a great Christian could be spiteful.

I mustn't omit Mr Moule who taught Latin and Greek. I gave up Greek fairly early but managed a credit in school cert, even overcoming the dreaded unseen. Mr Moule was very concerned with the correct usage of 'will' and 'shall' (I still agree with him). He used to illustrate this by quoting the Irishman who, attempting suicide in deep water, cried out, 'I *will* be drowned and no one *shall* save me.' It was Mr Moule who was the unwitting cause of my only beating by the Headmaster. It happened that Roden and I were in the sick bay immediately above Moule's classroom. It was around

5 November, and I had the idea that lighting some bangers timed to explode outside his window would be rewarding. As indeed it was; but there was a price to be paid.

One summer I went on holiday with the Parry family to Pwhelli in Wales; quite a journey in those days. I'd bought a small bivouac tent, fastened to the ground with metal skewers. (No inkling did I have then of the bivvies which awaited me a decade hence.) We set off from Forest Gate in the East End, in two cars. Alan drove one and I presume that the Revd drove the other. One was an Armstrong Siddeley – donated I believe by the grateful parishioners. I'm not sure whether it was that or the other one which duly broke down after panting up and down the steep hills of the West. I seem to remember that the AA arrived in due course, but I think it was a Big End, or something equally fundamental which necessitated a tow and repairs at our destination.

Some of the family slept in the farmhouse which was where we stayed. However, I and, I think, Roden pitched our little tents in the open farmland. It was quite cosy in my little tent, though the rain pattered rather threateningly on the roof. However, we survived the night and spent a splendid summer's day swimming, eating ice cream and all the wonderful things we used to do. (As did my own family on seventy magical holidays in north Cornwall.) My early diary which would have given chapter and verse of what followed has disappeared. Thus, I must rely on an increasingly unreliable memory. Anyway, on a later night an increasingly noisy storm blew in from the Atlantic. At a certain point, there was a sound of twanging strings as the skewers flew from the ground. My bivvie followed and I stood in my pyjamas, like King Lear in the black, tempestuous Welsh night. I think Roden had some difficulty too. Anyway we fled for shelter into the farmhouse. Next day the skewers were exchanged for stout wooden tent pegs and either the tent pegs or the weather improved for I believe we had no more nocturnal disturbances.

It must have been not very long after this that the Jewish question first arose. You must try to understand that, although I was vaguely aware of Jews and my unexplained connection to them, I didn't think of myself as having any religious or racial identification. This only began because of the anti-Semitic ramblings of the boy Hunter. He, together with two others, arrived one year when their previous school had closed down. When asked their names by a master, they identified themselves as Sir-Barnes-Sir, Sir-Mitchell-Sir and – my nemesis – Sir-Hunter-Sir. Hunter was large and had a shiny spotty face. He had joined Mosley's Blackshirts one holiday and

Sir John Paul (Jack), governing
the Bahamas.

thus became imbued with this Jewish antagonism. This all culminated in
insults in the quad, at which point to general amazement (and certainly to
mine) I gave Hunter the most tremendous slap in the face. He was both
literally and metaphorically stopped in his tracks; slunk off and waylaid me
no more. I think that it was this incident which has always made me more
sympathetic than perhaps I should be towards the Israelis, surrounded as
they are by their own Sir-Hunter-Sirs. Hunter finally disgraced himself one
Armistice Day ceremony in chapel by flinging his arm in a Hitler salute.
I was astonished a year or two ago in the obituary section of our school
magazine to read that Hunter had been a Hurricane pilot in the war. More
joy in heaven .....

Sadly, Weymouth College closed down after the War, being inadequately
endowed with money. I always felt that it more than punched its weight in
the world, and produced several illustrious old boys. In particular there was
Stuart Hibberd the chief BBC announcer whose dulcet tones declared in
1936 that, 'the King's life is moving peacefully towards its close'.

Also Squadron Leader Stainforth who in 1931 set the air speed record of 407 mph – the first man to exceed 400. We had any number of Knights, Admirals, Bishops, Ambassadors and so on; and an article was written somewhere expressing surprise that such a small school had achieved 26 Military Cross winners in the two wars.

Life was, by today's standards, extremely spartan. Terrible food; I still remember sausages whose origins today would probably be earmarked for dog food, and dainty canine noses would probably be turned up. We had one small pat of butter at breakfast. Porridge was stiff and lumpy ... well, you won't want a menu. And we were violent in a quite casual and really not psychopathic way. During my first week a boy who had sinned in some way was to be beaten in his pyjamas by one of the prefects. I watched, horrified as this huge man administered four of the best – numbers varied according to offence – to the victim. To my amazement the victim sauntered, smiling to the friends clustered round his bed. I soon discovered that it was a point of honour to show us no sign of pain however real it was. Dormitory beatings – always carried out with a hard leather slipper – were as it were our Coliseum – with prefects instead of lions. Word always went round early in the evening if there was to be pre-bed entertainment.

We spent all our money on food. We used to take a wooden tuck box to school (sent ahead by Carter Patterson and always delivered on time) and this supplemented the school food. Then there was the tuck shop, presided over by Sgt Bignell MM where in the morning break we guzzled huge (delicious) doughnuts. Biggy also sold stamps. I used to write home once a week, but never would have contemplated telling my parents what hell it was (for my first year) and what guilty pleasures enlivened the last.

Before I leave my school days, I should mention its keen interest in amateur dramatics. In particular I recall our presentation of R. C. Sherriff's *Journey's End*. I had to play an unwelcome role: Hibbert, the coward who is shamed by the hero Captain Stanhope. On the night, Peter Scott, quite a good friend who played the hero, got so carried away that he landed what should have been an innocuous fist on my jaw with such force that it knocked me to the ground. Ironically Peter spent the war in the Indian Civil Service; whereas I spent a good deal of it at the sharp end. Later he became Sir Peter, ambassador to Norway etc and also shared with me cataracts and angina. He, and his wife Rachael, both died in the early 2000s. Another good friend later knighted was Jack Paul (later Sir John). He got an MC for the heroic and self-sacrificial defence of Calais in 1940, was taken prisoner, and escaped only to be caught on the Swiss border. Jack was Victor Ludorum,

Weymouth College cricket XI. The author is in the back row, second from the left.

Head Prefect, Rugger blue, artist and general role model. He died in 2008 and his funeral was attended by a high powered congregation including a representative of the Queen. Jack's father owned the Victoria Hotel in Weymouth and I had lunch there sometimes. As a result of (I think) a Boer War wound, he only had one arm, but used to eat with a knife somehow shaped with prongs like a fork. One tried not to stare. After lunch we used to drive his large Austin around Dorset; long before I had a licence of course. But I had been driving – usually the girls' boyfriends' cars – since I was twelve. Jack married a schooldays admirer, a sister of one of the boys at school. They had three delightful daughters. Two of them took me out to lunch this year.

Then there was 'Waffle' – Sir John Waller, kinsman of the seventeenth-century poet Edmund Waller and no mean poet himself. He and I collaborated on a massive school chess tournament (jointly won by us!) and later at Oxford as co-founders/editors of the magazine *Fords and Bridges*. The last time I spoke to him he was living in the Isle of Wight with his (male) partner. I had never realised that he was gay. I usually don't. For example, I had a good friend, Frank, a fellow patient in the sanatorium (I'll come to that) who was Sir David Webster's (Royal Opera House boss) mate and whom I was always trying to marry off to suitable women friends. It was Frank who was told by Zena, 'Oh Frank you're so *gay*' before awareness set in.

At a certain point (probably after my first communion) I became rather religious. I asked for a bible for Christmas for example. My parents; what *can* they have been thinking; gave me a very nice one bound in red leather. It disappeared during my mother's destructive orgy after the war. Not, by then, that I very much cared but later have greatly missed it. I have one from Zena's family dated back to 1890 and with very small print.

The religious phase encompassed a holiday camp run by muscular Christians. We used to exchange biblical texts (usually that priggish little bugger, St Paul). I always sent Philippians IV, 13 – unlikely, if ambitious. Religion began to pall when I realised that – at least to the muscular ones – it mainly meant saying sorry to Jesus for masturbating. And, as the saying went at school: ninety nine per cent of boys admit to masturbating; and the other one per cent are liars. Of course we were warned of incipient blindness and hairy palms, but even these perils didn't act as much of a deterrent to the raging hormones of adolescent boys (and, I discovered very much later in life, girls).

In the summer of 1936 I did something which affected the rest of my life and put half a crown each way on a horse called Mahmood. It won the Derby at 100-6 and kept me backing horses ever since. In 1938 the Cesarewitch–Punch 100-8. In 1939 it was the Derby winner Blue Peter; and for good measure the Oaks – Galatea. After the war, my wonderful friend and betting partner Bridget Balkwill and I had some notable coups: notably the daily Tote Treble at Royal Ascot. The Balkwill family became important in many ways in the life of my family. But first more about racing. I have a file containing antepost vouchers, photocopies etc of some of my more notable successes. Unfortunately, I don't seem to have kept Mount Athos which came third for me in the Derby at antepost odds of 250-1 though the starting price was only – only! – 80-1. I spent some time before that race with Ron Hutchinson (later champion jockey) who was to ride Mount Athos and told him about my bet. He thought I was crazy. Many years later I backed Arcanges at 142-1 (pari-mutuel price) when it won the Breeders' Cup Turf in America. If you're not a racing person – or more likely if you are! – you won't want me to list some of the really long priced winners (and other bets) which have enriched my life and my wallet. But I did back Galcador at 25-1 to win the 1950 Derby. Also Red Rum in his first Grand National – and all his others. And in that race I had Last Suspect when it won. Antepost at

The author at Oxford.

50-1. Nor could I omit the immortal Brigadier Gerrard who obliged for me in the 2,000 Guineas at 10-1; odds never again to be seen for the great bay. There was another Cesarewitch with John Cherry at 25-1, Ginevra (16s), Juliette Marny (16s) and Sleeping Partner (16) in the Oaks and Droitwich Maid who won the Lincoln at 66-1. Of course, I've had my share of losers but between 1965 and 1995, my gross winnings were £7,045.

I still bet most weekends though in modest amounts. But a patent, which is three horses linked can be worthwhile. This bet, which I favour, and which costs me £2.80, has recently twice produced over £50 on successive Saturdays. My great racing break was when I was seventy-two. I had just lost my first retirement job – bookselling for eleven years – because the shop closed. Along came a young man from Darlington called David, who bought the premises for his Tipping service. As 'Computer Kid' he'd featured in the tabloid press, and made a lot of money. Anyway, he offered me a job – actually paying me for my lifelong hobby – and I spent the next three years, tipping, writing articles and doing a bit of broadcasting as Professor Pink. Alas, it couldn't last. David went peculiar and more or less broke, the firm closed after 3 years and I had about enough money to retire – for the third time.

Meanwhile, back to 1936 and Oxford. I made a rather unsuitable choice of college because Roden was going there and I liked the idea of sticking together. However, Keble, built in what someone called the Neo-lavatorial style, had been instituted for aspiring clerics; not a description which fitted me as I was already fairly agnostic and edging ever closer to non-belief. So Keble, high church in mood and endowed with an enormous chapel containing the original 1854 pre-Raphaelite painting by Holman Hunt called *The Light of the World*, was not really a suitable milieu for such a questionable Christian as me.

However, incipient parsons or not, Keble men were a hard-drinking, riotous collection, and I had no difficulty obtaining recruits for my first anti-social deed. The porter was a rather unpleasant jobsworth with whom I early crossed swords over some trivial matter. I decided that 5 November, Guy Fawkes night, would be suitable for retribution. My band of rebels and I each lined up in college windows with a bottle, loaded with a large rocket aimed at the porter's lodge. On the stroke of nine on the college clock, the blue touch papers were lighted, and a fusillade of rockets found their destination. A little later, an ally, Billy Simmons left a 'Grasshopper' which exploded 50 times. The porter was reputed to have come close to a nervous breakdown from that date onwards. The authorities had their suspicions and did their best to unmask the culprits, but security remained firm in my trusty, soon-to-be-dog-collared force; and the pursuit was called off. I did not do well at Oxford; mainly because I didn't do any work. Trying to cram a term's reading into one Benzedrine-fuelled night was not a success and in due course I found myself rusticated, or sent down for a limited period. This must have been a disappointment to my tutor, the famous Neville Coghill, who had an 'Oxford accent' whose drawl was as long drawn out as some wolf on the snowbound Tundra.

I did make a few good friends at Oxford – notably my best man, Roger, who also married a (very rich) Canadian heiress. He, like me, became a carer when Helen got multiple sclerosis and was increasingly helpless and died. Roger, too, has gone. I also became close (platonic) friends with a Dutch girl. She, her sister a rather glamorous art student, and their widowed mother lived in Orpington where I used to visit them. I had another friend who worked in the town. We spent exciting evenings on a stretch of the river known as Copulation Creek to which I punted with reasonable skill. After the war when Zena and I and Peter's godparents visited him in Cambridge, I once again tried out ancient skills, which brought me within a millisecond of a bath in the Cam. In the nick of time – much to the disappointment of my passengers – I let go of the pole.

Looking at an old diary, I appear to have had a university life devoted to drink and the pursuit of various women most of whom now mean nothing, for I can't remember anything about them. However, there are occasional outbursts: '...she didn't want to see me .... tosses me aside like this ... how could she do it? She has always been so sweet to me – so it seemed; I have learned better now. I wonder if I shall one day look back on all this as callow foolishness ...' This last was the only sensible comment; and, in 2009, how true!

That heartbreaker was apparently called Kathleen. More I don't know. Roden and I joined the Horse Artillery (in the University OTC). We learned about gunnery and to ride solo and in gun teams; all of which proved useful a few years later. I remember that we undergraduates used to admire in a terrified way a heavily made-up female predator called Millie Thwaites who used to hold court over coffee at Ellistons. She had a sort of fearful glamour which likened her to a Praying Mantis who would kill their mate after sexual pleasure was completed. We were all too inexperienced to try to test the validity of this theory. Millie was always known as a College Widow, a description used to describe a similar siren in the film *A Yank at Oxford*.

Once, Dad came up and took me to tea with Professor Gilbert Murray at his home at Boars Hill. Also there was General Crerar who commanded the Canadian land forces in the war. How Dad happened to know these illustrious people I don't know. I didn't realise at the time what a privilege it was. I was in my particularly obnoxious *fin-de-siècle* phase, and what they must have thought of this creature with his long hair and velvet tie is not hard to surmise.

My time at Oxford could indeed be described as 'the years that the locust has eaten' and in due course I failed my exams, was sent down and began to become what I hope was a more responsible citizen.

As I've mentioned women I should now describe a most beautiful raven-haired creature from Verona called Juliana to whom I became engaged (madness!) on holiday in Italy in 1937. We had to correspond mostly in French. In case you have unworthy suspicions: we were always heavily chaperoned and the nearest I got to her was on the dance floor of a holiday hotel in the Dolomites. Unfortunately – or do I mean fortunately? – the approaching war and my realisation that I had done a foolish thing led me to break things off in (I think) 1939. I received a bitter – and richly deserved - letter from this lovely creature but felt vast and unworthy relief.

Women! It seems I was always madly in love with one or other, so perhaps this is the point at which to describe how I lost my virginity; quite late in life by today's standards. Of course there had been 'necking' and 'heavy petting' as they called it, but I remained a virgin; a shortcoming (if you'll excuse the expression) that I felt keenly.

Anyway one evening in the thirties I picked up a quite pretty girl in a pub called The Alexandra. I had a car – borrowed I think – and we were getting amorous on the back seat, when she said suddenly, 'shall we?' Of course there was only one answer, but now that the vital moment had arrived, I wasn't sure precisely how to proceed. Hard to believe perhaps? Anyway I hopefully handed her a Durex which she rolled expertly on to me. And with her help found out exactly what to put where and duly climaxed in an intensely enjoyable way. At last! I was a man! I had DONE IT, and within ten minutes had done it again, this time without the condom and – what innovation – in another position. When I dropped my initiator home, she informed me that she was fifteen but obviously one of those promiscuous girls that boys dream about but rarely meet. (I hope the statute of limitations applies.) Women have been kind to me over the years, but there is always something unique about the first time. And though, next day, I felt that it had been rather sordid, a Rite of Passage had been fulfilled.

During the period 1937-39 when I crashed and burned at Oxford, I kept one of those Smith's Dataday diaries. On reading them as I enter the last part of my life, I realise what an unpleasant person I was: conceited, self-pitying and fickle. Maybe it was only the war which could prove my salvation and turn me into a reasonably decent citizen.

During my time at Oxford, and indeed until the outbreak of war and a bit beyond, I remained friendly with the Dutch girls from Orpington. They were very different in both appearance and character. Berthie had a dark complexion and brown, curly hair. Johanna was blonde, light skinned and rather more alluring. I was no more than a friend – a very close friend – to Berthie. We used to talk for half an hour on the phone and exchange views on more or less everything. With Johanna there was always a faintly sexual undertone. Berthie married an MP and Johanna a well-known thriller writer. Although Berthie had made a point of introducing me, I think she didn't want her sister to replace her in any way. I remember her telling me rather cattily that Johanna ate too much cream, was getting fat and had piles. But I do recall when going back to Dover after a few days leave, the very accomplished kiss that Johanna gave me at the train. I've tried without success since the war ended to trace these two friends. Unfortunately I couldn't accurately recall their married names.

I seem to have been involved to a greater or lesser degree with several women: Mary, my punting friend at Oxford; my unfortunate Italian beauty; a young North Country girl called Betty whom I met on a cruise in 1938. On this cruise on SS *Vandyck*, we had a very narrow escape on the 20

The author's father in the late 1930s.

September. About 6.30 in the evening during fog and rain a lean Romanian ship, the *Bessarabia*, suddenly approached us bows on. Its knifelike bows would have caught us amidships but suddenly it put on speed and swung broadside. Our vessel did what I think was called a quarter mile, stopped and swung away and the other ship just missed us. I was watching from the rail and could see the sailors rushing about on the stern deck. This incident was reported in the press (the cutting, alas, another of Ma's casualties) saying that the vessels missed by 50 feet. Of course, in those days ships had no radar and had to rely on lookouts and foghorns. Betty's aunt warned her (very sensibly!) against having anything to do with me after the cruise. Betty sent me a letter to this effect and I spent anxious weeks trying to decide what to reply etc. Anyway, after much correspondence it all ended, I seem to remember with a whimper and not a bang. Then there was Pam, the girl next door (to Andros) an unexpected late arrival and much younger than me. We got 'engaged'. All rather absurd and it petered out in a desultory way during and after the war. She was very pretty but not very bright. Finally, Griselda, but more about her later.

'I've been sent down,' I told my Dad, 'but I've got a job.' He goggled in amazement. On 4 July I wrote, 'Over supper I told them. It was a great shock but Dad really was wonderful. He said he didn't blame me and anyway it was "bloody" but it couldn't be helped. Ma was very upset but equally staunch.' They were admirable – it was more than I deserved. In fact, what I'd done was to go up to Fleet Street and – what cheek – simply walked in and asked various editors to take me on. One did.

CHAPTER 3

1938-39. *CAVALCADE*, KING'S COLLEGE AND GRISELDA

The man who took a chance was Mark Goulden, who edited the magazine *Cavalcade*, an unsuccessful attempt to imitate the American magazines *Time* and *Newsweek*. However, we did have one (enormous circulation booster) unique break when, presumably against all embargo agreements, we broke the story of Edward and Mrs Simpson. I think that we were regarded as pariahs but we didn't care! I was paid one guinea (£1.05) per week which isn't as grotesque as it sounds when you could get a 3 course lunch at Lyons Corner House, served by a 'Nippy' as the Lyons waitresses were nicknamed, for about 9p in today's money, and post a letter (there were 4 deliveries daily starting about 7 a.m.) for just ½ p in today's money.

I had a splendid time at *Calvacade* in Bouverie Street just off Fleet Street when I started on 4 July. I wrote lurid articles about drugs: 'Marijuana, the scourge of youth' and 'Galveston, Hell city of the South.' And I reviewed films usually going to press showings in the morning. I became quite hard-bitten about films. For example I only watched with an indifferent smile when Spencer Tracy in *Captains Courageous* told Freddy Bartholomew 'Don't cry little feesh.' Nowadays the most maudlin soap operas have me welling up. And as for the Remembrance Day march past ...

One story I did was to write up Jack Doyle's Training camp – Butlin's at Skegness. He was a handsome but not very expert Irish heavyweight boxer. I interviewed him and a number of other people from whom I gathered that the young lady campers queued up outside his chalet most evenings. When I wrote the story up voicing my doubts about Doyle's prospects with ironic references to the local slogan, 'Skegness is so bracing', Mark said he couldn't use it because of the advertisers (I suppose Butlin's). Jack Doyle's next bout was not a success. He was knocked out in the first round.

In these days, when I can Google or email in search of almost anything, I am very aware reading these diaries of how many letters I always seemed to

Griselda (left) and Ursula
Todhunter.

be writing. And the recipients tended to respond with pen and paper. I think
people did correspond more in those days; although by comparison with
our Victorian forbears we must already have seemed quite laconic.

I think I had regarded my job at *Cavalcade* as a defiant gesture to the
world, i.e. Oxford, which had rejected me. Anyway, as advised by Russell
Meiggs, the Dean of Keble, I had applied for a place on the Journalism
Diploma course at King's College, London and had been accepted. This
course, the only one of its kind I believe, was run by Tom Clarke, ex-editor
of one of the national dailies. The work suited me well, my output was good
and I was told by the Dean that because the war curtailed the course, I was
not able to be awarded the Gold Medal for which I was the front runner.
Very ego-soothing after my earlier academic performance. I heard that the
Dean told the father of another student that I had done 'brilliantly'. At
King's, once again, a very remarkable woman entered my life; and stayed
with it, for long after we were both married she invited Zena and me to
Polesden Lacey where she lived because her husband, Ivan, was the top
man for the National Trust in the area. How impressive to sit on Edward
VII's mahogany loo seat! And to move freely the other side of the ropes
which prevented tourists and other lesser beings from exploring *our* part of
the house. Griselda Todhunter was beautiful, eccentric, neurotic and very
intelligent. She was one of three girls whose father, a learned professor, chose
to converse mainly in Greek. Her sister Ursula was even more beautiful but

not especially clever. We called her The Bolter, because like Nancy Mitford's Linda in *Love in a Cold Climate* she was always running away with a different man. The third daughter, Angela, was rather unfairly condemned to anonymity by these exotic siblings. Griselda (often called Grizzel or Griz) was my *Belle Dame Sans Merci* for she certainly had me in thrall for a year or two. But to be fair to myself it was by no means one-way traffic. I notice in my diary for 5 April 1939 that 'I made love to her in a restrained way, and she said rather an odd thing suddenly "I wonder why I'm so terribly fond of you ..."' Griselda and I were something of a triangle with a man called Richard Picton. Once, she told me, just to annoy I suppose, that she had made a suicide pact with him. On 19 June, the following entry: 'Incidentally I asked G yesterday "Has Richard ever kissed you?"' (a stupid thing to do I realise seventy years later!) She said 'Jack, you ask such unfair questions'. I take it Richard has. I am surprised as he has bad breath – is, I consider, rather repulsive physically – and because I shouldn't have expected G to let him'. Poor Richard always had a premonition that he wouldn't survive the war; he was a pilot with Bomber Command – and he was proved right. To sum her up: one entry reads, 'I am looking at G's photograph and my God she is beautiful.' But another; 'I hate G because she has shattered my peace of mind; I hate myself for letting her; I hate her for her flirtatiousness, her petty interest in gossip and intrigue; I hate myself for being spotty and run down; in short I think I hate everything tonight, but chiefly myself.' Griselda died of cancer in 1985. Her son Tom told me. My niece Monica called her favourite doll Griselda Todhunter and I remember her with unbounded affection.

At King's, I enjoyed a mildly sophisticated reputation. I was a little older than most of the students; had been sent down from Oxford; had worked in Fleet Street, the Mecca of us all, and had a rather snazzy little car – a silver Sunbeam Talbot. Though the most important, Griselda was not the only girl who entertained affectionate feelings towards me. Of course, all this was after what we all knew as The Munich Crisis in September 1938. I think that like most people of my age, my attitude to war had been affected by the aftermath of The Great War. There was an ingrained pacifism, a feeling that it must never happen again. Bé had a picture book with harrowing pictures; this was a city, this was a wood etc. The one I most clearly remember showed a corpse riddled with holes from a machine gun. The caption: 'This was a man'. Some diary entries: '27 Sept Time marches on. It really looks like war now. Chamberlain made a really fine broadcast to the nation today at 8pm and it seems clear we stand by the Czechs. As we should, I think. So now we can only await 1 October with calm and steadfastness for it looks like the end. We are ready this time anyway so now it is the turn of the Flower of 1938 to make the world safe for democracy.' On 28 September I note that Hitler has invited Chamberlain, Mussolini and Daladier to a conference in Munich. 'Can they come to agreement tomorrow? The world waits to see.'

'30 Sept And so – peace. And a very complete and all-embracing peace (10 points) according to the communiqué of the Munich conversations. Poor Czechoslovakia ... but I suppose that even if you criticise and detract from the peace, it still is peace and that's a lot.' Craven but typical of the way most of us felt.

1938 dragged to its end. There were lectures at King's. I remember that I found Economics 'an extremely dull subject – even if half the dons at Oxford and Cambridge have written books about it – or perhaps because!' It may also have been that the lectures were given by Hugh Gaitskell – dreadfully boring and not to be guessed at as the future, rather inspirational Labour leader. I was horribly susceptible to girls – especially Berthie, the bewitching and troublesome Johanna, and even Dora the beautiful but stupid and totally unattainable next door widow with whom Roger, later my best man, *was* infatuated. I was singled out by Tom Clarke – one of three – at the Practical Journalism course. All the others had to rewrite, but I was getting A, A and A – even at my poorer subjects. I read all of George Orwell's books, indeed I still have a first edition of *1984*.

By then, it was Spring and 1939 and I had my desirable Sunbeam Talbot. It was also the time of trial with Griselda who bewitched and tortured me. Looking back now, 'all passion spent', I can scarcely credit the heaven and hell of my green and salad days; but on balance, I think Tennyson probably had it right with 'better to have loved and lost than never to have loved at all.'

More often too, I worried about the increasing likelihood of war. My exams had gone well and I found a job as a reporter on the *Wimbledon Borough News* – a strange portent of days to come. My work didn't pinpoint me as the next James Cameron. The editor would send me out to 'do a few deaths', which usually involved bothering distraught relatives. Once I did a story at Dr Barnardo's. But, as I say, nobody cried out, 'hold the front page!'

My twenty-first birthday was on 15 March, the day Hitler marched into Prague and began to dismember Czechoslovakia. Poor old Ides of March. In 1936 the previous week had seen the invasion of the Rhineland and probably the last time we could have prevented the Second World War. I

noted that I had about 6 Greetings Wires and 2 others, as well as about
10 letters, a china dog, 100 Three Fives cigarettes from Roger, a Mason
Pearson hairbrush from Nag (still with us) and Flo, Lizzie's broadly Norfolk
successor. Champagne for supper and Dad gave me £5 – over £200 in today's
money. How I remember that large white note signed by Mr Bradbury; the
first one I'd ever owned.

I spent a very self-indulgent summer of 1939. Long drives into Kent, new
clothes, among them a tailored sports coat and Daks trousers which cost
about £1.50 in today's money; much more expensive than most – Guinea
Guards for example. I used to buy them at Simpsons in Piccadilly. Manicures
at Austin Reed where my regular was 'Bluebell'.

Towards the end of August came disaster when Griselda mangled my
psyche by ending our friendship because 'we bored each other'; though –
typical this – she promised to get together again in October if there weren't
a war. As it happens, I did see her again in 1941 when she was in the WAAF.
We went to Cheltenham for a weekend and by evil chance met Johanna,
staying in the same hotel. Johanna had a civilian job (BBC I think), looked
glamorous in civvies and made Griselda furious because the WAAF uniform
did nothing for her. The weekend was not a success.

At the beginning of September London had the blackout. All cars had
masked lights making driving difficult. On 2 September I drove home (to
Andros) in a torrential thunderstorm. 'The lightning,' I noted 'was almost as
bright as daylight'.

Next day – Sunday – Chamberlain announced at 11.15 a.m. that we were
at war. At 11.30 the air raid sirens sounded and we prepared ourselves for
the obliteration we had so long been given to expect. It was a false alarm.
So was the one at 2.55 a.m. the next morning. We assembled in the cellar
of blacked-out Andros. I think that the presence of The Master was almost
more alarming to Flo and Nag than the prospect of bombs. The Master only
went downstairs at Christmas and was a figure of awe. I remember he told
me next day, 'I was the calmest person in the house.' I began to ruminate on
my destiny as the day I was to enlist (as a volunteer) drew near. This was
the time of 'the Phoney War' and I hoarded petrol before rationing started. I
flirted with casual girls, hoping to drive the omnipresent Griselda out of my
mind. On 13 September I went to Oxford to enlist. There is a strange entry
in my diary on 4 December: 'Nothing to write tonight. Am feeling terrible
but will not tell even my diary why ....'. What on earth was that all about?

During November I was working again at *Cavalcade* and I was living at
Andros – a feather in my cap as Mark was turning applicants down. I note

The author, 1945.

that I had written a feature on yoga, had 82 inches of copy one week and had been to a press showing of *On the Night of the Fire* which had a school friend – Terence Young – as Assistant Director. He introduced me to his guardian, Brian Desmond Hurst.

Terence became a rather well-known film director. An early success was *They Were Not Divided* – a David and Jonathan story based round The Guards Armoured Division. He also directed several James Bond films including *From Russia with Love*, considered by many to be the best. At school he was a very good leg spin bowler (we played in the same First XI) and a full back who, I think, got a blue at Cambridge (Jack Paul, unluckily, just missed his). I was also selected by Mark Goulden to compile a booklet containing 10,000 facts about the war.

I read Masefield's *Gallipoli* and wrote that it, 'has some exquisitely lovely passages, particularly when they sail from Mudros and all the ships cheer and cheer because the young men are so beautiful and brave' (poor bastards ...).

I had extensive dentistry with a general anaesthetic because I couldn't face going into the army with so much to be done. Lots of extractions, a new plate, much misery. (Shape of things to come in '43, '44, '45.) My (not very capable) dentist was Hugh Bruce-Payne, one of Elly's suitors. Very tall and handsome but not the fastest-revving drill in the steriliser.

My time to enlist drew near. I was still writing a good deal for the magazine. In my diary I cite a long story I did on a German 'Freedom' radio station. I also note some rather jingoistic songs on our own radio: 'Red, White & Blue, What Does it Mean to You?', 'There's Always Been an England, and England *shall* be free!'

On 13 December 1939 I left *Cavalcade* with much regret. The Boss said I could come back any time; and at the time I thought that was quite possible. Next day I made my last entry ..... 'I think I shall be killed, I always have – but maybe I'm wrong. Goodbye.'

CHAPTER 4

1939-43. SOLDIERING

I suppose I'd assumed that I'd be given an immediate commission when I joined up. After all, I had passed the (ludicrous) army exam Certificate A at school and been in the OTC at Oxford. So, after passing the medical A1 at Oxford on 10 September 1939, I was dismayed to discover that I was to be an Other Rank. In the event it was one of the best things that ever happened to me; my callow, snobbish outlook would have made me an unsuitable officer. Later events and experience in the ranks helped to make me what I like to think of as a good one. But that first pip lay a long way ahead; and its justification even further. Meanwhile in December I joined my field training regiment in Dover in the coldest winter in 100 years. Twelve foot snowdrifts and a frozen river Thames.

In Dover, we lived among snow drifts as high as sixteen feet and temperatures I was not to experience again until the Ardennes battles of 1945. In the frosty early morning moonlight, clad only in shorts, we bent and jumped at PT. By day we learned the rudiments of gun drill and ballistics on our ancient world war artillery pieces. Inefficiency attracted punishment such as running round the barrack square with a 25 lb shell held aloft. To the Regulars – old sweats from India – this sort of discipline seemed normal, but to us, soft civilians, it took time to get used to. In the end one saw the point: discipline – which made our peacetime army so good; and, I suppose, made soldiers of us too.

Every week we paraded for our pay: 10p a day in today's money. I spent most of mine at the Sally – the Salvation Army; a paradise of hot baths, egg and chips and kindly ladies. The Sally remains today a charity which I regularly support. I had my hair cut really short when I joined up. At our first parade the Battery Sergeant Major looked at me and barked to a subordinate, 'get that man's hair cut!' My neighbour, inadequately shaved, was told, 'your face is covered in *shit*!' Yes, it was a harsh regime but like prison not unduly testing after public school life – as Jonathan Aitken, a recently incarcerated minor aristo affirmed. My new companions and I eyed each other a bit warily for the first few weeks. (They were baffled when I took off all my clothes at bedtime and put on pyjamas.) However, class divides were soon forgotten and I was accepted as 'us' in a shared hatred of 'them'. When later I too became one of 'them' I was able to identify with my first military mates and had no difficulty with the all-important code that their welfare was always to come first.

A fellow gunner I have never forgotten was called Eric Stenton. I think that he must have been what we later called a fellow-traveller – or even something a bit more subversive. In the army he played his guitar and taught us all disrespectful left-wing songs. A verse of one of my favourites claimed that, 'We Germans have no room to pee in so we must have Colonien' and its rousing chorus line: 'I ain't going to grieve my Aryan whore,' repeated three times. There was also 'Andrew Smith' who 'did my share of the dirty work when I was a Soviet worker' – a parody of one of the Left-Wing Book Club titles published by Victor Gollancz. Eric and I re-met at my house after the war but he always remained a rather elusive figure who died before I could start a serious look into his life and his link with Andrew Smith .... 'As I walk around the Red Square with a nonchalant sort of air, you can hear the girls declare he must be a commissar, but I'm laughing up my sleeve because they never would believe that I'm the man that does the dirty work for Hitler' (to the tune of *The Man Who Broke the Bank at Monte Carlo*).

The best efforts of our ferocious ex-India Army NCOs only tended to make us as bolshie and work-shy as possible – specially on an occasion such as Christmas Day 1939. I was on duty that bitterly cold night with a chap called Mike Liddell. We were both supposed to be selected for officer training, but both turned down by the CO – Colonel Rendell (a.k.a. The Pessary). I met Mike in the Western Desert in 1943; both of us officers, he even RHA. Luckily we were not called on to repel the might of the Wehrmacht as we plodded round with our elderly Lee Enfield rifles. No, we raided the cookhouse and stole several large turkey legs, left over from the sumptuous Christmas dinner. We demolished them smugly settled by a warm stove. It was probably the most comfortable if not the most martial, of my seven army Christmases.

This also applied in another context: church parades. The Sergeant Major; 'RCs, Parsees, Push Baptists and Sun Worshippers one pace forward *march*'. I refused to be classified and possibly had the army's only Hindentity discs as my Sergeant called them, stamped AGN for agnostic. I still have my discs

– one green (to be buried with you in the unfortunate event that ...) and one red. You wore them round your neck at all times. I was offered the choice: Church parade or cleaning out the latrines. Proud – even at this late date – to say I stuck to my guns and became an efficient cleaner.

Although not deemed worthy of a pip, I did achieve a Lance-Bombardier's stripe, and – I can't remember exactly how in late summer it came about – found myself at a place called Dyce in northern Scotland marching a large squad past a very senior officer, roaring out 'eyes r-i-i-ight' and throwing a smart salute. He must have been baffled. Whether this had any bearing on my selection for officer training I don't know. I was trained as an OP (Observation Post assistant), learned to ride a motorbike and, just as the (false) alarm rang out for a suspected invasion, lay in a tent in Scotland with pneumonia. I was determined to get to OCTU (Officer Cadet Training Unit) and my mates procured me oranges, and from a friendly chemist M & B 693, a powerful new drug with which I overcame the illness. I managed to skip parades and presented myself – weak but willing – at the OCTU at Ilkley. The friendly MO hearing my story put me on a tonic regime of strychnine tablets (one a day up to fifteen) which seemed to put me right. Just as well, because the OCTU regime was just as exacting as Dover, with the added, never far out of mind, terror of RTU – Return to Unit if found wanting.

It was there that another of my Jewish episodes occurred. The CO to whom I reported was Colonel Sebag-Montefiore. Thanks to the ignorance of my upbringing, I simply had no idea that his was one of the most eminent Jewish families in England. So I was rather taken aback when he barked at me, 'Are you a Jew?' I explained my background in a fumbling way which can't have impressed him.

I made close friend there: Denis Carter. It was he and I who used to call the Lord 'Murphy' following the Irish squaddie who referred to 'Chassus Murphy'. I added a verse to *Away in a Manger*:

> I love thee Lord Murphy
> I ****ing well do
> And I don't care who knows it
> Cos it's ****ing well true.

I also wrote a poem (to the tune of *Three Little Fishes*) about the three majors who ran the OCTU:

Jock Cochrane.

> There were three little majors
> At a little OCTU
> Dobrée and Todd and Tickety Boo.
> 'Shoot' ordered Dobrée, 'Shoot if you can'
> And we shot and we shot to a fine fire plan.

I can't remember what the third major was called, but anything that met with his approval was 'tickety boo'. And finally I rewrote a well known song as follows:

> When you come to the end of a perfectly bloody day
> And your minute cows moo with pain
> You look at each other and then you say
> Tomorrow's the same again.

(*Minute cows*: a certain NCO always used to pronounce 'minute' (very small) like the unit of time. So a minute cow was a calf; and the calves ached with marching etc.) Denis, alas, died of cancer in the sixties. We never lost touch, and once he took me flying in his tiny little Auster. Just like sitting in a small chair in the sky. I loved it.

I did, finally, survive the OCTU and emerged in 1941 glorious in my Sam Brown and single pip. I can't pretend that I swayed the tide of battle during the ensuing years but I served under one Jock Cochrane, a kinsman of the famous Admiral. Jock became another of my role models. He sported a monocle and a dry wit and such was my admiration that I applied (successfully) to join his battery when I was posted to the Desert in 1942. He greeted me in a sandstorm as casually as if we'd been parted for a few days. It was a devastating blow when he was killed on the Libyan border on 13 February 1943. (Two years later to the day, I was wounded.) I wrote at length about Jock in the Diary I started on my way to the Middle East. When I made my last entry in Germany after the war ended, it had filled seven closely written volumes. I did make desultory and unsuccessful efforts to get them published. But at this point they were stuck away in an old ammunition box in the loft where they were – unknown to me – submitted by my great-nephew Simon to Alan Sutton and published by him in 2005, with a paperback reprint following in 2007. I've drawn extensively on this Diary in describing my wartime service. Reading it sixty-five years on, I am amazed that I found the time – and energy – for it. As I told Simon, it seems to be about somebody I used to know very well. Now, in my increasingly limited old age, I have to respect my youthful endurance.

I had met Jock when I was posted in 1941 to 132 Field Regt in Dorset. I can't say that I did anything very useful that summer or in 1942 except train and ride a motorbike many dusty or rain-drenched miles as our convoys traversed the West Country. We got to know a houseful of FANY (First Aid Nursing Yeomanry) officers in Milborne Port near our camp and spent convivial evenings with them. I was tasked with finding food for the mess and became a talented scrounger from the St Ivel factory in Yeovil to which I sped on my BSA or Norton motorcycle – the hand throttle open as far as it would go, whisking me through the Dorset hills at 75 mph – no crash helmets in those days.

The battery clerk was a pale, bespectacled and thin young Welshman with extreme talent for mimicry. Later he became rotund and knighted. Little could one have guessed in 1942 at Harry Secombe's successful life. I was rather friendly with a subversive subaltern called Gerard Tallack. We secretly mocked the 2 i/c, an ineffectual Regular who referred to the Red Army as barbarians; and an unknown diplomat called Sir Reeder Bullard, a resonant name which we used to boom out at each other. Jock's verdict on Gerard: 'talented but impossible.'

I can't say I've any clear recall of my time in 132 Field but as summer 1942 ended, I was moved out of the regiment along with other, not vitally useful subalterns and put on a draft of reinforcements to the Middle East. We had to collect shorts and other 'Tropical Kit' including a pith helmet which may have been *de rigueur* in the Transvaal in 1900, but which we discarded from Suez onwards after derisive comments. Our living quarters in Woolwich, home to the gunners, were quite Victorian – dusty, dirty and ramshackle. The day came when the train took us to Liverpool and a Dutch ship called the *Sibajak* on which we travelled round the Cape of Good Hope, *en route* for Suez and the war in the desert. The *Sibajak* had served the Dutch East Indies and the ship's stewards were small, nimble Javanese who served us food only to be dreamed of in austere, rationed England: delicious white bread baked on board, veal and other tempting meats, butter in generous quantities. The air grew warmer, the sea more blue, and flying fish accompanied us as we sailed southward. The *Sibajak* was rumoured to have been sunk on her return journey, but in fact survived the war carrying troops and emigrants, and was finally broken up in Hong Kong in 1959. I have told you of my meeting with my brother Dick in Gibraltar – our last encounter until after the war. We docked in Durban, where, drinking with George Long, our RC *padre*, large, worldly and unsuited to the cloth, some mates and I spied an unbelievably pretty blonde girl at another table. Nobody else would make a move so I (what an opinion I had of myself!) strolled across and explained that we were all entranced but only I had the courage to ask her to join us. This was Moira Lister, later a very well known actress who would become one of my lifelong friends. She married an utterly charming French nobleman – Jacques, Vicomte D'Orthez. He had a bad stroke and Moira nursed him for four years in their home in Cadogan Square. At his funeral service I met one of his daughters – Chantal. Moira eventually returned to Cape Town and my son Richard visited her in Constantia where she died in 2007.

George fell in love with Moira and I always thought he had seduced her, but no, she told me, 'I was a good little Catholic virgin.' She was shocked by George, who in today's parlance came on to her. He wrote a book called *All I Could Never Be* after he left the priesthood (or was he ejected?) In it he mentions a young subaltern called Jack, who advised him of his unsuitability for Holy Orders! George joined the chindits and had an adventurous time in Burma. I still have a sketch he sent me of the Persian Desert. Like all who knew her, he was totally charmed by my wife Zena.

In Durban, I wrote a longish satirical poem called *The Convoy Cutey* about some of the predatory but unforthcoming young ladies of the city.

The Convoy Cutey, or You Have Been Warned

None but the brave deserves the fair, 'tis said.
It seems to me that this should now be read
None but the rich in certain ports of call,
Where if you're poor you have no fun at all.
Toll for the Brave, the Brave that are no more,
They met disaster on a distant shore ...
They weren't struck down by bomb or sabre stroke –
The Convoy Cutey got them and they're broke.
Savage at night, rapacious in the day,
The Cutey combs the clubs in search of prey,
Like Dracula through crowded streets she floats
Gorged not on blood, but crackling one pound notes
From Pilot Officers and Second Lieuts
Who scented hints of much forbidden fruit.
But when they peeled the fruit they found their slip –
No fruit for them – they only got the pip!
The Cutey knows the City's snuggest haunts,
The Cutey likes the most expensive jaunts,
The Cutey sips her tea in deep armchairs,
The Cutey's interest in taxi fares
Ceases, when after evening well spent
She speeds a chastened captain towards his tent ...
Damn it, she shook his hand before he went.
(He ought to think his money's been well spent –
Next thing you'll say she should have kissed him too,
There's too much sex in nineteen forty two.)

Toll for the Brave; they've empty wallets now,
And all the money that the banks allow
Has vanished utterly. I've heard them say
'If this is pleasure, hurry up the day
When duty calls. It's simply that we feel
H.E. is safer than this sex-appeal.
Though Germans don't wear lipstick, we agree,
You must admit they entertain us free.'
Frailty, thy name is Woman – who said that?
Let me tell you he's talking through his hat.

In certain cities where the convoys ply
Concrete thy name is Cutey would apply!

Soldiers are simple stuff to hypnotise –
You merely drop some Stardust in their eyes,
Then get the band to put slow foxtrots on,
And pretty soon his next month's pay is gone.
You charge him double for the drinks (worst brand)
Perhaps unbend, and let him hold your hand –
But make it clear your heart lies with another
(You simply look upon him as a brother,
You'll find that works.) And when you've had your fun
Rolling your eyes and hips at everyone,
Look at your watch, say 'Lord, it's nearly one,
I must go home or Mother dear will worry –
Apologies for such a tearing hurry.
I'd like to ask you up. I can't; I'm sorry.
Don't see me in, the nights are very damp,
Goodnight, good luck — and don't be late in camp.'
(And if he doesn't ask you out next night
Why worry; there are plenty more who might.)

Cuties about in all seductive guile ....
The lifted eyebrow, and suggestive smile.
You'll see them sitting over tea or grill
Looking for somebody to foot the bill.
Lithe are their figures, and their waistlines neat,
Slender they look — but heavens, how they eat!
The only uniform the Cuties wear
Is evening dress and sleekly waving hair,
Their feet are neatly shod — but here's a scandal,
No silken hose is eased into their sandal,
Their only stockings are the ones they pour on,
But after all (don't say it) there's a war on.

Toll for the Brave. Three years they've passed through here,
Hoping to find a sympathetic ear.
They who expected such delights in store
Tottered North gratefully, to find a war

In which two fairly equal sides could play!
Butchered to make a Cuties' holiday!
They were a sort of human Lend and Lease,
They were a modern type of golden 'fleece'.

At Sundown, when the bars begin to fill,
The cuties don their warpaint for the kill,
In all the little flats that are their dwelling,
While in the lounge some wretched stooge is telling
A hawkeyed mother how he likes this part,
And realising with a sinking heart
That when he brings his Cutey home at night
That female buzzard will be there all right,
As though to say to him 'Escape me— never!'
(Be cute sweet maid — and let mamma be clever ....)

Toll for the Brave. I'm tolling for them too.
As Churchill said, it's seldom that so few
Have paid so much. But hell, there's nothing new
Beneath the sun; and Cuties will abound
As long as sex-starved soldiers hang around.
'Long live the war', the Convoy Cuties cry,
'Let 'em all come — we'll have a damn good try
To clean 'em up. Eleven bob a day
Is not much dough, but this increase in pay
Which we have heard may soon be coming in
Ought to provide an extra spot of gin .....'

Don't be downhearted, ladies, if my verse
Should make the sucker situation worse.
The time will come when we shall sail away,
And pretty soon will come another day
When Cuties rush around and cry, 'It's true –
Boatloads of bulging wallets are in view!
Out with the cars and glad-rags — what a sin
To waste a minute; let the Trek begin
Down to the Docks! Another Convoy's in!!'

Moira broadcast it on South African Broadcasting Co. and somewhere in North Africa. I received a cheque dated 10.12.42 for 8 shillings (40p) which I recently found among my relics. Quite an imposing 9 x 5 it is made out to 'J Swarb'. (I feel that *Convoy Cutey* may not be up with Alexander Pope or even Clive James, but it still reads pretty well.)

Another Jewish episode in Durban. With Harcourt Summers, an ex-*Sibajak* chum (always called Debroy like the bandleader) I visited friends of my father's – Mr and Mrs Caplan. We were invited to lunch when I should have known – but didn't – that heads were covered when grace was spoken. In the event Debroy and I had to put table napkins on our heads as this strange chanting took place. We didn't dare catch each other's eye. Mr Caplan figured in another incident in my life. Debroy and I and a few other mates from the *Sibajak* became friendly with a group of girls with whom we bathed at the glorious local beaches of Isipingo and Amanzimtoti. Sunbathing one day with a blonde Afrikaans girl I quite liked called Valerie, I was a bit taken aback by tears and a tale of woe. Some US serviceman had put her in the family way and sailed north. Please could I help? I, who'd been in the place a week or two!

Anyway, I sought out Mr Caplan (who naturally took me to be the impregnator) who produced a doctor's address. Valerie was rid of the unwelcome addition; I was regarded with disfavour by my hosts. Val gave me a copy of the *Rubaiyat of Omar Khayyam* in which she had written, 'To Jack, the best friend I ever had'. I carried it with me always, until it was stolen from my haversack as I lay zonked out on morphine after I was wounded a couple of years later.

After a few blissful weeks we sailed for Suez on the *Oranje*, the newly built flagship of the Rotterdam Lloyd line. By coincidence I had planned a holiday in 1939 which included a maiden voyage to Algiers on this very same vessel. On this occasion, however, it was crammed with troops, some ground staff RAF officers (uncharitably known as Wingless Wonders), some WAAFs, nurses and a few civilians. A fellow officer, David Roberts, and I did a turn at one or two of the concerts we gave. We called ourselves the Middle Eastern Brothers after the Western Brothers, a UK duo. By a strange coincidence after the war, I gave a job to Patsy, one of David's daughters. I wrote the lyrics – poking fun at everything official – and David played the piano. Among the civilians was the wife of a diplomat (soon to be an ambassador). 'M' was the object of the lustful longing of all males on the ship, including need I say, me. Possibly it was the wittiness of the lyrics but whatever the reason, I was the one that she desired. As almost every corner of the ship was occupied, it was hard to find somewhere we could get together. Eventually one dark night on the dark deck, 'I'm thirsty', she said. I wasn't sure where I could find her a drink. Silly me. We did manage a few other trysts, generally in the bathroom of the cabin she shared with some nurses. Once, just as we docked, the anchor was dropped with an enormous crashing sound.

When we got to Cairo, I occasionally got away from the camp at Almaza and joined M in her room in Shepheards Hotel – one of those famous imperial hotels like Raffles in Singapore and the Taj Mahal in Bombay (in both of which I stayed later in life).

I remember our standing naked exchanging intimate looks in front of a full length mirror. She told me she was 2½ months pregnant. Admiring her delectable breasts I made some appropriate comment. 'You know too much', she murmured fondly as we returned to her enormous double bed. We spent some memorable evenings in a city where entertainment was, let's say, unusual. I don't think I fully appreciated how lucky I was. When I left for the desert, a tearful M gave me a St Christopher medal on a silver chain. It was engraved *To JS from MM Dec 1942*. I have it to this day. I remember she gave it to me as we embraced in a small space in the centre of the great Pyramid of Giza; one of several excursions we took while I awaited my call to a desert unit. I liked Cairo immediately and always have done on several post-war business trips. There was a certain smell ... oriental spices and petrol engendered I suppose by the warm climate – wonderful in the winter-time, which it was on that first visit back in 1942. It was paradise for the staff officers, who lived in luxury and were despised by the soldiers who had served or were about to serve in the desert. They were known as Groppi's Light House (Groppi's was a splendid restaurant in the city) and the Gezeira Lancers. They were of course a permanent feature of Shepheards Hotel, guzzling the peanuts with which the staff ensured a supply of thirsts which had to be quenched. (The staff in Brussels in 1944 used to wear the Shaef (Supreme HQ Allied Expeditionary Force) badge on their uniform. We called it the Cross of Shame or sometimes The Red Badge of Courage.)

There were swarms of small boys all over the city and transit camp, imploring you to let them clean your boots and avail yourself of other services ('my sister very pretty jig-a-jig'). There were lots of brothels – strictly off limits to the poor soldiery – and nightclubs – where I saw my first belly dancers.

I had a letter from Jock Cochrane on 23 Dec 1942, promising to rope me in if possible and on Christmas Eve came my posting – to 127 Field Regt in which he commanded a battery (491). I had a fearful cold but managed what I described as, 'a bloody good Christmas dinner of traditional make up,' and the next day set out, with a draft of 92 disgruntled men, for the regiment – having previously met Jock's Battery captain who promised to see the CO and get me posted. The journey to my unit – by boat and truck was extremely uncomfortable. I mention one of my fellow travellers whom I describe as 'a young rather Rupert Brookeish type' commissioned directly from Cambridge. He was one of two that I remember who was sent back out of the line in tears during the fighting in Holland. I discovered later that he'd been promoted to Major in charge of a POW camp.

This is how I arrived at the Regiment – whose last adjutant I was to become – on 3 January 1943. 'I am writing in a terrific sandstorm (in a truck). We are 7 miles West of Alexandria. And I've got Jock Cochrane's Bty. Not a good day to arrive, but they managed to scrape up 2 cold sardines and a cup of tea for lunch which we ate under a tarpaulin since carried away by the gale. This sand is simply terrible, gets in everything and one's eyes, mouth and nose are choked right up with it. It's bloody. This is said to be about the worst they've ever had, so it's a good introduction. Jock is the same as ever and was pleasantly unimpressed at my appearance!'

Life in the 'Bluey' as everyone called it – a sort of cynical nod at The Wild Blue Yonder - was extremely Spartan. Our only food was either bully beef or m & v (meat & veg; nobody asked what meat) and hard tack biscuits on which we spread some anonymous fat we called axle grease. Also the army supplied us, rather surprisingly I thought, with ascorbic acid tablets; a source of vitamin C – and our only one. We had a mug of tea morning and evening and sometimes in the middle of the day. At one point the water came from some salt marshes and made the tea taste horrible – 'cricket's piss' it was called, an odd description.

Ablution had to be achieved with one enamel mug of water, or more often a 50-cigarette tin. Skilful use of a shaving brush and a toothbrush enabled one to shave and rinse. Shaving and washing was mandatory – a form of discipline which was always observed. We didn't want to look like the Italian soldiers, unshaven, scruffy and given to excreting anywhere and leaving it uncovered. We were very strict about that. When we were on the move, which was more or less always, and no latrines could be dug, we would take a shovel, dig a hole and squat over it. Afterwards the hole had to be filled in – to the disappointment of the black, armoured 'shit beetles' which tended to fly into your face as you squatted; usually in the gloom of late afternoon. Night fell rapidly and all around stood hundreds of men peeing as the cold struck their kidneys. Nights were bitterly cold with a heavy desert dew. Early on I had no tent and just crawled under a tarpaulin which quickly became soaked. Sleep was more or less impossible. Later, I used to have a doovah – a small trench – sometimes with a little bivvy tent above with two levels. You slept on the first and left your boots etc (when you could actually take them off) on the floor below. Boots had to be shaken before re-use to remove the scorpions which tended to nest in them. We became thin and brown and remarkably fit considering our inadequate food and liquid intake. It was a mistake to get a cut or a graze because – owing to the dry desert air, people said – they were difficult to heal. I acquired a splendid batman – Tom Findlay, who stayed with me until he left the army a couple of years later. In spite of all its privation, I grew to like the desert; specially at night when the sky was full of stars – so much brighter than when seen from the city and you could hear the sea breaking on the shore in the still of the night. Also, apart from the two armies there were few humans about; Arabs selling their tiny eggs and an occasional emaciated lamb. We exchanged these for tea and 'eggies for chai' became the accepted commerce. Later, we used to put a layer over used tea leaves but were soon rumbled by people whose need to live in lonely places had sharpened their wits. Our lambs had their own slit trenches as we didn't want them prematurely slaughtered by enemy shellfire. And there was a certain attitude of respect towards this enemy, perhaps because we knew they shared similar conditions. We got to know certain formations – the 90th Light, the 15th Panzer Grenadiers – and, indeed, the Africa Korps itself, whose desert equipment was so much superior to our own: dark glasses for example, and binoculars, both of which I acquired in due course.

So, with my new regiment, I advanced westward during January and February 1943 towards the piper-led victory parade in Tripoli past its well-known landmarks: 'Marble Arch' – Il Duce's vainglorious monument near El Agheila, 'Edinburgh Castle' near Homs, where, one night, I saw Wimberley, the Divisional Commander, rush up to a small artillery unit crying out 'throw shells, throw shells!' Not exactly precise instructions. We were under fire occasionally, but nothing as alarming really as my experience of the Blitz in London, when, on leave and stricken with 'flu, I lay listening to the whistling and crash of nearby bombs in Eaton Square. My greatest personal sorrow was the death of Jock Cochrane on 13 February 1943. Looking back as an old man, I find the feeling I expressed in my Diary entry, and those for days to come, a bit surprising. I thought I was a bit of a cynic in those days and Jock was not so much an intimate friend as admired role model. However, I

Diary entry 18 November 1944.

was clearly racked with sorrow; shades of Arthur Hallam and those distant days with *In Memoriam*. For example, this is what I wrote on 14 February:

Last night I lay awake for a long time thinking of Jock, remembering him vividly even down to the exact sound of that sort of snorting chuckle he used to make when he was amused at something. I remembered a discussion we had on biscuits and their effect on teeth when he said in his allegedly callous way 'some of the weaker brethren gave up the struggle and had to be removed.' I remembered what he said when I was complaining to him one day about the lack of a proper job – 'Oh well one of these days somebody'll go on a course or to hospital, or get himself killed ...' And then I realised again that he had cracked his last cynical joke. He was probably the best soldier in the Regt. I didn't realise till he was dead how much I also thought of him as a man and as a friend. So I lay there for hours staring at the Plough in the clear bright sky and feeling an overwhelming loss and sadness. And now I shall have to get used to doing without him. Today we are still in action the same place and unlikely to move till tomorrow as the other 2 batteries have gone forward. It is cold and sunny with a gusty wind blowing up a bit of sand. It is like all days in the desert.

As I say, my experience of enemy fire had not been extensive, but that changed on 17 March, two days after my twenty-fifth birthday, with its Diary entry, 'Devoid of Incident. Beware the Ides of March?' Two days later, tasting battle for the first time, it was far from devoid of incident. This is how I described a night I have never quite forgotten:

Yesterday the first stages of our attack – nibbling at the outer Mareth positions – went in. I had asked to go forward with Alistair as FOO to gain experience and give a hand and eventually the BC said I could go. Now, I lie in bed writing this in the quiet and wondering if the events of last night really occurred or were some awful nightmare – however: We left here at 6.30 p.m. and by about 9 had reached the infantry debussing point. There was a bright half moon and the night was noisy with our guns whose flashes could be seen round the horizon. Later the Boche air force joined in, bombing back areas by the light of bright yellow flares. All this was the artillery preparation for the Guards and 50 Div who put in the first attacks. By 23.00 we were up at the FUP where the Germans started shelling us fairly violently. Luckily, we were in the middle and most of them fell just right and left of us. At about 01.00 our Vickers opened up with a most devilish pandemonium, firing across the valley we had to cross. Overhead our shells were singing towards the ridge we could just see – our objective – and enemy shells and mortar bombs fell among us. Once I heard a man screaming and sobbing as they scored a hit. I put on my tin hat and lay flat. Eventually the infantry (and my god, what guts these boys have got) went over the ridge and were driven back by m.g. fire but went on again, and we went after them with our cable reeling it out on foot. Then the fun really started. They were shelling that valley quite hard. Once we were lying flat and if you imagine we were the centre dot of a domino 5, we had 4 all round us about 20-25 yards away. They don't whistle when they get close but make a kind of screaming hiss which is very frightening. I found a Gordon with his leg badly smashed by shell splinters. He was lying there in the smoke and cold so I gave him my coat. Later I managed to get a couple of stretcher-bearers to him and thus got my coat back. The bearers were as gentle as women with him and I realised the goodness as well as the evil in men afresh. Soon after this our artillery put down an ill-conceived smoke screen, which in the still night failed to rise at all, and soon we were groping and stumbling along in a dense fog which made us cough and stung our throats. I don't know what time it was when we crossed the Wadi Zeuss and got into the gap in the enemy minefield. Time lost its ordinary values, even tho' I did check it frequently on the luminous face of my watch. The minefield gap lay just the other side of a marsh and was a thin lane marked by white tapes and lighted by tiny lights which seemed to shine like beacons. Two Scorpions – the converted Matildas we use for clearing gaps – lay like huge unwieldy beetles, stuck in the bad going. Three machine gun posts stammered in front of us in the fog of smoke and the bullets buzzed and whee-ed over our heads. On the right – a mine went up and I heard for the first time that curious wailing cry, 'Stretcher-bearers!' and again the groaning of the wounded. Sappers were everywhere, taping and picketing the gap; they are brave and efficient. But bravery in battle is a curious business. It certainly is not accounted brave to be foolhardy, and when shells are flying, you see people lying flat and making no bones about it. I believe that we suffered casualties around this point – I suppose it was about 03.30 by then and we were feeling tired, cold, and footsore and craved a cigarette which we couldn't have. To cut a long story short we were on our objective soon after 04.00. In the gloom figures poked about with tommy guns and bayonets. The moon was just going down and it was getting dark. Here we left Alistair (who, I discovered, is a good calm leader, tho' he hates every minute of it – and no wonder after going through this sort of thing with every attack) and began to make our two mile journey back. Before we got to the FUP we'd walked about 4 miles and I was beginning to feel tired. Some of the signallers were weary and a bit jumpy so I made them walk slowly in single file which helped. Just before we re-entered the minefield, our lives were probably saved by one of those strange twists of fortune one reads about. Our carrier (the OP) had torn a chunk of cable out and we had to mend it. I was impatient at the delay, but a minute later there was a blinding flash and concussion as though somebody had hit one on the chest with a heavy book. In the middle of the 'safe lane' a Sapper had trodden on a B4, largest of all the mines. When we reached the point, he was lying on our cable with one leg blown off. A minute later and we should have been there too, as were picking our way back by going down the line. Two of his friends were trying to comfort him, tho' he was hardly conscious. 'Never mind' one was saying 'you'll be alright, you're out of the war now, you'll be going back to Blighty' – all the things men are supposed to say. Now I know that they do. It was getting quiet now, with only the enemy guns shelling the whole area. Our tired little procession stumbled back, every now and again flattening out as shells landed near with that harsh, shattering explosion they make. Bombardier Lambert was a good influence, and stayed very steady. The journey back was, in a way, worse because you knew that once you got back there was a cigarette and a meal waiting and you so desperately *had* to get back. This feeling easily leads to a mild panic and that's why I made them walk slowly and in formation. We lost the wire this side of the Zeuss crossing but luckily I found my way and about 05.20 just as the first signs of light appeared, we got to the FUP where I reported to the colonel, very deep in advanced RHQ. At 07.00 we were back on the gun position. I went to bed at 10.00 and slept until 17.00.

As the war went on I experienced many and much more personally dangerous occasions, some of which I'll describe, but it would seem that one's loss of military virginity resembles its sexual counterpart. When we liberated Sfax on 11 April it was our first taste of public cheering, flowing wine and flowers thrown by pretty girls. 'We have waited, it seems, so long', one Frenchman told me, 'and we knew that only the Eighth Army could save us'. I spoke to a Russian Lt Col acting as a war correspondent, whose complete set of gold front teeth gleamed in the sunshine, and asked him what the Russians think of us. 'The Eighth Army very good; the rest – civilians in uniform but you are learning, you are learning ...'

As the victory in Africa drew nearer, I was doing quite a lot of OP work. In particular I spent a bad day at the Djebel Garci – a feature in the hills at Enfidaville known as The Bleeder. This OP had been a German one and therefore had to be occupied and left in darkness. This was my entry for 26 April:

> 1200 – This OP was known as Garci Feature (or Djebel Garci): Relieved Alistair about 01.00 on the morning of 25 April. Hell of a climb to the OP which is perched right on the peak of a well registered (ex Jerry) hilltop. The OP being blown in (and it must have been as near a direct hit as makes no difference) it took signaller Kelly and myself till first light to mend it. Caution was enforced by Spandau bullets. I don't intend (being tired) to go into details now except to say that we had 80 105mm shells in the area yesterday which was no sort of fun, specially as about 10 were so close they filled the OP dugout with splinters and fragments. One large piece hit my tin hat and knocked me a bit silly. I took on an enemy mortar OP 400 yards or so across the valley as a close destructive shoot (our own troops being just below it) and got my gunfire on target. Was glad to leave the bloody place, lost our way and got here almost weeping with nervous exhaustion. A few shells down the line then a quiet night. Good chit from 'Good Show' Harben.

When the fighting ended at Cape Bon, I was sent on a mission for some luxuries. With Findlay and my driver I motored over large sections of Algeria, meeting various characters – US Colonels, Senior ex-Fascists etc, and at Ebba Ksour completed my mission laden with 10 bottles of whisky,

6,000 cigarettes, 600 razor blades and 468 bars of chocolate. I noted that 'lack of money presented large scale activity!' At Souk Aluas the Town Mayor placed me in the Grand Hotel d'Orient. 'In honour of my real bed and running water', I wrote, 'I am about to don my silk pyjamas. I have washed my feet, eaten well and am about to sleep a great sleep'. (In the winter war in Europe, I often wore the silk pyjamas under my uniform.)

At the end of May I went on three very drunken days' leave in Algiers and returned to await our next task, which we knew to be an invasion but we weren't sure of our destination. My taste of active service had evidently changed my attitude, for I find that, as we awaited our fate anchored off Sfax, I wrote: 'I remember now, before I'd seen action, I used to say I wouldn't mind dying etc. Since then I have realised how callow and essentially unsound were my words. Life has become (even in its worst moments) very sweet, and I certainly *do* mind dying now. This makes me fear that I shall; it seems to be so often the case.' We only discovered that our destination was Sicily at sea on 9 July just before we ran into a ferocious storm. Our flat-bottomed LST rolled alarmingly and I was extremely seasick for several hours; so much so that, next morning, driving our waterproofed jeep in three feet of water towards Cape Passero, I felt only relief at the prospect of dry land – bristling with enemies or not! My first entry was on 12 July: 'Last night when I lay down under the stars, it was exactly 39 hours since I had slept at all.' That rather typified the thirty-nine days of the Sicily campaign: the first glorious grape-laden vines, peaches, pomegranates and oranges; scarcer as we drove north. The water – so abundant after the desert – and the heat – 120 in the shade and dust which coated us as we advanced. I had by now been appointed CPO – Command Post Officer, in effect co-ordinator of the eight guns of our battery. Sometimes it was like this (on 24 July):

Tremendous flap last night when the enemy counterattacked about 10 o'clock. Not very usual for the Boche, who doesn't seem to go in for night attacks in a very large way as a rule. However, after a burst of firing and a slight local withdrawal, things became quiet again around midnight. I quite like the Command Post in the middle of the night. It is quiet, and only the hushed middle-of-the-night voices of the signallers, the occasional buzz or ring of a 'phone, and the sounds of instruments and pencils clinking round the artillery boards break the silence. Somewhere behind Etna's formidable grace a German gun bangs flatly in the night. The moon shines on the yellow cornfields and shows the mountains shadowy and vast in front of us. Everybody is rather tired; the small electric bulbs and hurricane lamps glow harshly on strained eyes. We seem alone in the world, marooned, a small technical island in the infinite complication of the night.

Somebody brews up. We sip the stuff loudly and with satisfaction making the invariable remarks about the incomparable qualities of tea, which always accompany a brew – particularly at night.

When morning comes and the daylight shows up the untidiness, the tired unshaven faces, one wonders that midnight could have touched the scene with mystery and almost romance.

There was some sharp fighting at Sferro (where there is a stone monument to the Highland Division which had over 1300 casualties). I attended the last rites of one of my gunners on 26 July and wrote:

Today I went up to the farm area we occupied near Hill 199 the other morning when Barries was killed. I was with Alistair and the Padre who gabbled an extremely perfunctory 'few words' over the small grave with its rough wooden cross. The hot sun (it was 120F in the shade yesterday) beat down, a breeze from the sea carried the thump of guns and shells to our ears, and the droning of the Lord's Prayer mingled with the stern voice of Spitfires overhead as gunner Barries' earthly remains were entrusted to his alleged maker. I'm afraid I didn't find the scene as touching as I should have found it. Rather pointless. I'm sorry I did but there you are. Passing 301's old position four more crosses mark the place – and a fifth is since dead – and all around is the desolation of empty gun pits, burned trucks, paper flapping in the wind, and the black scars of the hillside where the shells have fallen.

As we moved in August our advance continued northwards. The days were hot and humid – sometimes 105 at nine in the morning – and by day twenty-two tempers grew frayed. On 1 August we attacked with 150 guns from 23.50 to nearly 02.30. I wrote:

At 2350 the guns duly crashed out and the night was loud and hideous until nearly half past two. During the barrage I went outside to have a look at things. The night was dark save for the continuous flashing of the guns. The reports hit you in the face like a blow. It is almost impossible to think, let alone speak. Later the Boche started shelling back; though we had no casualties there were some rounds in the Battery area. Two of the crew of the Bofors protecting our position were hit, one dying on his way to hospital. On 304's position, a gun pit which had caught on fire flamed and exploded for hours, lighting the bare hillsides. A few flares hung in the sky, and occasionally a bomb or two thumped in ahead of us. At 03.00 I fell into bed but was up before 05.00 since when we've fired nearly 800 rounds. It is now 22.15.

On the night of 8 August we fired 250 rounds per gun at such speed that a captured German officer asked to see our 'automatic 25 pounders'. By 15 August the Germans had left. We moved up to Messina and to the intense interest of the locals, prepared the guns for the barrage which was to accompany the attack on the mainland. So it came about that on 3 September – exactly 4 years after the war began, I wrote the following:

> Never in my now reasonable experience of gunfire have I heard anything to equal the monstrous blast of our guns last night. The doors strained and blew open, windows smashed, ceilings fell in and the command post wall disintegrated by slow stages. First the veinous crack, then the chip falling out and finally great chunks of plaster cascading on the floor in clouds of dust. By the dismal grey light of dawn our village square was a sad spot, all the house stripped of plaster and cement, every window smashed and roofs where no tile was left intact. Dazed and deafened we sipped a cup of tea afterwards. The landing is a success and already the airfield south of Reggio is in our hands. This morning the sky is full of our bombers – Bostons and Mitchells, twenty-four at a time sailing in tight formation with the bright sunshine on their wings. Over the straits the first barrage balloons are beginning to blossom exactly like early snowdrops.

After this, we had finished fighting for the time being and we spent much of the next two months on some delightful leave. I bathed in sun-drenched surf and met several very pleasant Americans – particularly Lootenant Katz – who took us to their PX (the Post Exchange – a very superior Naafi) where we bought shirts, shoes, torches and various foodstuffs. 'Gee, I get a great kick out of hearing you guys talk', said one of our hosts.

Sicily had had some of what these days we call scary moments. I remember one evening towards sunset in mid-July. We were in convoy on a mountain road when I suddenly saw six Messerschmitt approaching. As I watched, their wings seemed to twinkle with lights. Something told me to drop under a wall by the road. Just as well as a hail of lead howled onto and over us and we had quite a few casualties. Luckily the 109s continued on their way home.

In September another Jewish episode in my life. Our revered Divisional Commander 'Tam Tam' Wimberley was appointed to the Staff College. I met him once during a night skirmish at Homs. He was a very large, impressive figure. On 17 September we were drawn up in the sun and addressed by the new GOC. In my diary I describe him as '.... unprepossessing. Slight, with rather protruding teeth, a somewhat rattish face ...'. However, in an earlier paragraph, I had written: 'Here is the passage which struck me as most significant. He was discussing the hero type of German sneak-raider which shoots down Brighton High Street "kills off a few dozen people and drops two 500 kilo bombs which knock down a couple of shops – *which probably belong to Jews anyway."* This sally failed to rouse the applause which apparently was expected for it. I was amazed and disgusted at the bad taste it showed ...'. This general, Charles Bullen-Smith, never empathised with his officers, the Division lost reputation in Normandy, and on 26 July 1944 he was told by Montgomery, 'You must go, the men won't fight for you. You will go home now.' The general was in tears. Montgomery, deeply moved, added 'If I don't remove you, Charles, men will be killed unnecessarily. You must go.' (Bullen-Smith had been a staff officer in the 3rd Division of the BEF commanded by Montgomery.) I have quoted the details of his dismissal from *Monty's Highlanders* by Patrick Delaforce. I remember at the time, with *esprit d'escalier*, I wondered what would have happened if I'd called out, 'You're wearing the wrong uniform, Sir.' Presumably court martial, reduction to ranks etc. Another *esprit d'escalier* has lived with me for years. Dozy with pre-med at one of my operations at Guy's Hospital, I am wheeled into theatre where a rather pretty young anaesthetist takes my hand and, readying her syringe: 'just a very small prick.' Oh the missed opportunity, the lost witticisms. Alas, no young doctor has given me a second chance.

Yes, not all our fellow officers were kindred spirits. One evening in October my truck had broken down so I had to stay at the military government HQ – a pleasant villa. I saw a large Lieutenant who resembled Goering, shouting at some Italian servants and hitting them quite brutally. (Ashamed to say I said nothing.) Among those present, I noted at the time:

Lt Ted Marshall: An ex RASC Lieut, rather lumpen and with no teeth, they are being repaired. Quite affable. It was he who first extended the invitation.

Capt Bill Hare: An ex-Detective Inspector who talks a lot but quite interestingly. A baldish rather sinister man. Very friendly.

Major Sir Charles Buchanan: An amazingly pukkah relic from the HLI at some time in his life. A regular. Very much so. Service in the East y'know and last

Bill Carney.

war ribbons. Changes for dinner – of course. Is rather horrified and puzzled by the other two. Don't know if he's a Bart or not.

My relief truck hadn't arrived by the next evening: '....I went out to dinner with a local princess who spoke English well. Dinner served amid tinkling glass and silver. Dinner was soup, fish, joint and sweet, preceded by vermouth, accompanied by wine, red and white, and followed by champagne, coffee and liqueurs. So much for poverty stricken Sicily. After dinner, two gloriously lovely girls came in and spent the rest of the evening. When I got back, the wagon had arrived, and next day we went back'.

All such a poignant contrast with those months in the empty desert. Then in mid-October, great news: we were going home early in November. I was rather ill and feverish at the time but duly recovered enough by 30 October to describe our evening entertainment as follows:

Yesterday we all sallied forth in the evening to see 'Sicilian Follies', a display at the State Theatre by some local ex-lovelies. The theatre was crammed full of sweating gunners chewing nuts and clamouring for sex. From every box they overflowed, and the high balconies were a sea of faces. Eventually amid roars of applause the curtain rose and four or five rather faded trollops started waving their fannies at a highly appreciative audience. The show followed fairly orthodox lines. There were the 3 youngish dames who weren't too bad to look at. One aroused considerable speculation by wearing a brassiere throughout the evening. Bill Carney thought she had false breasts, but popular opinion decided that, on account of the generosity of her bosom, it was a measure to prevent it popping out. (This, incidentally, was a turn in itself and evoked about 4 encores.) There was an apoplectic soprano who sang *Madame*

Butterfly and *Ave Maria* with every vein bursting out. There was the local tenor who looked like rather a seedy edition of George Raft and sang with throbbing emotion and scant regard for the time. Later he reappeared in a pair of black trousers about 25 round the bottom and hitched up under his arms, and a pink shirt, and beat on a tambourine and cavorted round the stage. The audience was puzzled but polite. The comedian relied almost entirely on sex and scored something of a hit. The show wound up by a two woman scene, one being dressed as a male, and singing lustily they performed antics of an extremely sexual nature, with much indecent caressing and undoing of fly buttons. What they were singing I am unable to say – as it was drowned in the roars of applause.

CHAPTER 5

1943-44. BACK TO ENGLAND. CLARE

And on 11 November, we sailed – in a convoy of 6 ships on SS *Argentina*, a quite modern 22,000 ton liner (American Republican Lines).

Meals on board were served twice daily at 08.30 and 18.00 on large airline-type trays so absolutely loaded with food that the interval seemed if anything too short. A sample supper: *hors d'oeuvres*, soup, fish, enormous dish of pork and veg, pudding, ice cream, cheese, fruit and tea. No wonder some people felt a bit seasick when the waters got rather rough off Cape Bon. I thought it was a fine sight and wrote: 'During the afternoon, the sea got up and in a headwind with the tremendous seas rolling against us, the convoy battled through the misty afternoon. Occasionally the sun broke through, and I saw the silver grey gleam of the escorts – fragile ships leaping effortlessly along. The spray exploded against the sunshine and shrouded the ships in cobwebs of colour. It was a magnificent and significant spectacle. As always, I realised afresh the far-reaching power of a maritime nation, and was struck by the beauty of the ships thrusting their bows against the living ocean.'

In November, it grew cold and many people used to life in the desert, were poorly with colds and coughs. On 25 November we docked in the misty Mersey with a promised fourteen days' leave, our HD signs worn again, and our Africa Star with its little silver '8'. We arrived at Amersham at 01.37 with, 'Fog this morning with a clean November smell – lovely.' Hard to sleep, thinking of home and leave.

What a memorable leave that was in Christmas '43 and the days that followed! We knew that we'd been described as 'elite troops' by our desert foes, and, brimming with 8th Army pride, were undoubtedly disliked by troops who'd been training the UK for the larger task we now all faced: the Second Front, as it was called. We knew that we'd been brought home to spearhead the invasion into Europe and I sometimes had uneasy nights thinking about the reception we were likely to receive at the Atlantic Wall. It was then that I met Jock's widow whom I shall call Clare, using the third of her three names. She it was who was to occupy my life – and my heart – for so much time to come. I invited her to a regimental dance and proudly introduced her to people who'd served with her husband. She wore a vivid red evening dress. I was enthralled, helpless.

The south east corner of England that spring was one vast military camp. Tanks, guns, trucks, dump of ammunition in every corner. I noted in my diary the many unfamiliar Divisional signs – a pointer to the size of the operation which lay ahead. We were inspected by Monty. By the King. I motorcycled as often as possible to hasty meetings, and unwelcome partings, with Clare and her small daughter, born on the last day of 1942. In my introduction to part 3 of *Field of Fire* I noted: 'We didn't know our precise destination; and thanks to an ingenious deception plan, neither did the enemy. The Intelligence people initiated fictitious radio traffic indicating the presence of an (imaginary) army in south east England, complete with inflatable dummy tanks, trucks guns etc readily available for aerial photography. A manmade harbour had been constructed, to be served by Pluto – pipeline under the ocean.

All this was unknown to us ordinary soldiers as we waited to open the Second Front. It was to be very unlike our recent battles.

And many desert veterans would not see their homeland again.'

I remember I did feel apprehensive and noted 'I never can think of myself as a veteran'. By the end of May we were shut in. Excerpts for the following days give you some idea of the atmosphere as we prepared for the coming ordeal.

Hot today: makes this place a vague reminder of the marshalling area at Sousse; particularly the way the dust spurts up from the paths as thin as talcum powder. We do PT stripped to the waist and sweating like pigs ... I suppose it's over 80F in the shade today – and we had some sort of steak pudding for lunch – god!

I feel I am well prepared for *this* invasion with over 800 cigarettes, 3 lb of slab chocolate, tea, milk and various other amenities of life which were almost unknown on other parties; curious to think this is the third similar occasion.

The hot camp – more like Stalag – daily presents a veritable picture of resigned boredom. Men are lying about nearly naked, sunbathing, or gambling either at solo or throwing pennies. The glare here gives me a headache. It's an odd feeling to be shut away like this with 'civilisation' (meaning hot baths and phones) so near the perimeter.

Idle thoughts pass through my brain as I lie on my bed. I flick my cigarette ash off and it explodes like a little silver bomb in the sunshine ...

The barbed wire is lined with half naked men commenting vociferously on the passers-by. Girls on bicycles get rousing cheers, anything representing authority, from our armed guards of the Queens Regt to motor cycle cops, a volley of boos and catcalls. Outside the camp there is a pond in which we wistfully watch brightly clad civilians having a bathe. A pity they could not have extended the perimeter a little, then *we* could have used it. Meanwhile our interests centre almost entirely on such animal comforts as *are* available such as cool showers, packets of (very good) fruit drops made by Needler's; and much hot tea; also the newspapers.

Almost nothing has happened today. A piece broke off one of my teeth today and I have to go to the dentist tomorrow morning. It always reminds me of that chap Watson who was killed on a bike recently. When I saw him all dead and bloody I noticed a lot of his teeth were stopped and thought of all the pain it must have caused him and what a waste it had been.

The dentist told me that this camp brings him so much work that he's praying for the Second Front to open. 'One man's meat ...'

Soon after ten: I am lying on the duckboard floor of my tent. Night is falling fast. The door of the tent, not the usual open one but the one opposite and facing NE, is open. In the near distance the trees have lost their full summer green in the evening mist. The tents are drab and brown. Slit trenches with their mounds of gravel scar the ground. The concert party nearby warbles *Tea for Two*. When the comedian is on, laughter surges across the camp with the rhythmic regularity of surf rasping on a shingle beach. It is hard to realise, lying here in these last few hours of peace, that soon I may be hearing the waves on a real beach, and the sound of gunfire, flares by night, the crunching crash of bombs and the moan of dying.

With these hours of strained waiting we are paying for those wonderful hours of anticipation when the Argentina lay safe in the Mersey and the gulls wheeled about us and it was misty and cold and raining – and home.

3 June. 14.00: We are sailing down the Thames on our Liberty Ship from East India Dock.... The ship is unbelievably loaded with trucks, stores, rations – and men. Everybody is stowed in a hold aft with no room to swing a cat, but some of the ship's officers have been very good to a few of us, and I've been superbly lucky enough to get the couch in the Chief Steward's room. This will make the trip instead of a sort of floating Black Hole quite enjoyable. There are no washing arrangements except for a few buckets, and sanitation is almost non-existent. Meals, composed of compo rations, have to be eaten where a

bit of space can be found to do so. In this cabin, however, I've no complaints. There is a radio which can be played till we leave anchorage and a desk at which to write this, and running water. What more could one ask? If these are to be my last few hours they will at least be comfortable ones. Amazing as we swung down the grey Thames this afternoon to think that two years ago I was at Woolwich also waiting to go overseas. How life passes ...

I was talking to L/Bdr Kelly in the Naafi last night. He said when we mentioned Jock's name, 'Christ, I wish that man were back with us now,' little knowing how closely he echoes my own thoughts.

As we sailed down river towards the boom and the flak towers beyond it, we passed an enormous gathering of all the different kinds of vessel required for the invasion of an enemy coastline. I saw LSIs – the ex passenger ships whose lifeboats are now assault boats, and from whom the Commandoes steal forth in the darkness; and troopships; and then like one of those old-time ballroom dances a huge line of LSTs, each with its barrage balloon floating above it. And in between the grey 'little ships' slid about the grey river – MTBs, corvettes, destroyers and gunboats. And others – more sinister like the rocket boats – which I didn't recognise.

Finally the waiting ended, and on 6 June I wrote:

It is 08.45 and we are sailing for France. No details except that we were supposed to leave at 4 and actually didn't until about 3 hours after that. It is a crisp clean morning with sunshine and on our starboard side we can see Kent. The corvette next to us sent a message that we were bombarding Le Havre and in his opinion the party had started – midday – and we are just about at Dover harbour. The chalk cliffs dazzle in the sunshine but a strong wind is blowing, and it is cold. Eastwards down the channel stretches the long line of grey ships, with little escorts bobbing among them. Across the water I can see Calais shrouded in mist or smoke. A few Spitfires fly above us, their lines as slim and beautiful as the gulls around the vessel. But so far no breath of action, not a sound from the enemy 20 miles away. Can this really be the invasion? It is so far like Sicily all over again. The wireless is silent so we know nothing at all. We are passing Dover now, and I can see the barracks beyond the castle where I was stationed 4 years ago. The mate has just told me the radio has announced that landings have been made – shells and explosions outside – I shall go and have a look see.

12.15: Shells from France. One Liberty ship behind us on fire. Escort laying screen. Everybody to wear tin hats.

13.15: Later this ship which we thought at first to be the one with the rest of the bty on it, blew up with an enormous pillar of flame that plunged over 200 feet into the sky. It wasn't the ship we thought, though. The damage was caused by German shore batteries in France. It was the very thing needed to add a touch of reality to the situation. Realising that the ship was only two behind ourselves shows how very close is the margin between safety and danger on these occasions. We have just passed Folkestone where Clare's father is Naval O.i/c. I wonder if he saw the incident?'

We spent the night of the seventh on our LCT (Landing Craft Tank) just off the beach surrounded by burning ships, green fire on the beach and some bombs which were uncomfortably close. Early on the eighth we made the 120 yards to Sword Beach in water three and a half feet deep; but a cushy enough situation compared with the slaughter of the Americans at Omaha further down the coast. We pushed on inland in clouds of dust past wrecked tanks and fallen comrades, past minefields (*Achtung Minen*) and huge poppies, wild roses and peonies. I had bad headaches and 'took too many Veganin'. There were bombs and active snipers but generally tolerable conditions until on the eleventh when I took a recce party inland from Hermanville with a view to setting up a Command Post. Unfortunately this was in full view of the German OP, in what became the notorious Chimneys at Colombelles which, I believe, defied every effort of gun and plane and survived our advance eastwards. I didn't envy the FOOs manning those chimneys, though on our first acquaintance we didn't enjoy the 150 shells with which they greeted us – many being 88 mm airburst – very unpleasant. I noted that we 'withdrew', which was a military description of the speed with which we got the hell out of a nasty spot. The first few weeks in Normandy were a new experience for us after the open desert. Here the rain, the snipers and the narrow lanes of the bocage all held real or imagined menace. Sent on one occasion to Battalion HQ, I was told on arrival that the village (Escoville) we'd just passed through was full of snipers who had shot up our predecessors. It was in Escoville that I recorded seeing some wild-looking women – 'half crazy' I wrote. We were able to treat ourselves with some luxuries – butter, cream, cider and eggs from the farmers, in exchange for soap, candles, bully beef, chocolate, razor blades. However, the rain and wind and of course the attentions of the enemy didn't make for a pleasant life and I'm not surprised that I opened my Diary on 19 June with, 'God, what a bloody miserable day. My CP team had become skilful scroungers so early days among the crashed gliders of the 6th Airborne Division had yielded up excellent booty such as seats and electric light bulbs; all of which made the command post more comfortable. Also, my soldiers had, by now, faith – largely misplaced – in my judgement. This was inspired by an action I took on 14 June, which I described:

02.05: I am in the new CP – the one I had dug by bulldozer (for an emergency) the other morning. The reason is as follows. At about 23.00 the usual nightly raid started; heavier than usual tonight. Eventually it culminated in a stick of bombs right across us, the last precisely *5 yards* from the Dutch barn under which we were located. It blew a good hole in the road and the barn roof collapsed in a shower of tiles. Splinters flew in and punctured one of the trucks, some petrol tins, water tins, and brew cans. Two hurricane lamps smashed. Miraculously had no casualties. At least, I say miraculously but some intuition (or was it?) had made me uneasy this evening and much to everybody's irritation I insisted on moving tonight and digging out and finishing off the hole. So nearly everybody was (as we were in the middle of moving) able to get to the ground. We are actually just behind the barn and showers of everything fell on us. Otherwise I don't like to think what might have happened. During the day enemy have shelled the area quite heavily, particularly towards evening.

Yet here is the first sentence on 15 June: 'Uneventful day; hardly any enemy shell .... had half a chicken for tea and looked just like Henry VIII.'

We were having quite a large number of casualties, particularly of course the poor old infantry. I mention 5th Black Watch, with whom, did I but know it, I was soon to be so familiar, and whose officers I so admired. I want to give you an impression of what the Normandy bridgehead was like. Here is my entry for 20 June:

23.30 Command Post: Tonight I paid (for this evening) my second visit to the real front across the canal. It is a sinister little world across there, of deserted villages – or what remains of them – and the broken relics of war machines and men. The OP was in a barn roof and I spent some time there. The farm was also deserted, only a few very neutral-looking civvies are left in it, with slatternly hungry looking children. And the grounds are thick with mines. There were some gardens there, all overgrown, with weeds encroaching on the onions, and geese and hares moving about quite unmolested. Over a concealed slit trench sprang a great bush of huge red wild roses and some other flowers the colour of bluebells, which I did not recognise. And over everything hangs the quietude of death and danger, broken only by the sound of shell bursts or machine gun rattling.

In front of the OP cultivated fields and tidy hedges. Farm houses, and on the horizon (which is a near one) a thick wood where the Germans are lying. In front of the wood are a couple of knocked out tanks, but I don't know whose. I think his. In front of the OP are two dead cows, already swollen and legs stiff in the air like upturned rocking horses. All the nearby villages are smashed and the desolation fills one with amazement and sorrow. This is Herouvillette, which both sides wanted. Over by the bridge (Benouville bridge) going back, a Jeep (I was also in one) had been hit. By the roadside lay those bundles one begins to recognise so quickly, covered with blankets, and still forever. Driving back in the twilight I shivered ....

However – and I always felt a bit guilty – four days later my time in Normandy ended, when I was found to have raging malaria along with many others whose tablets taken in Sicily had finally lost their effect.

CHAPTER 6

1944-45. WAR IN EUROPE

I was in the OP at Herouvillette, feeling like death and with an almost literally blinding headache. I'd eaten nothing except Veganin since the day before. There had been mortaring but generally fairly quiet except for the morning when the enemy put a smoke screen in front of us and out of it emerged an armoured car firing an automatic weapon at the OP. Everyone opened up with Bren guns, rifles etc but I remember that I felt so ill I was quite indifferent to the din. When I left the OP I saw Dr Dewar, our regimental MO. He found that my temperature was 104 and sent me to the MDS, where they filled me with quinine, took a blood slide and decided I had malaria. I lay on my stretcher listening to the guns and bombs and at dawn I was carted, still on my stretcher, to the CCS, standing for Casualty Clearing Station near the beach. More bombs, then to an air evacuation centre, and we bumped and jolted about 16 miles to an airstrip, where I was loaded into a Dakota and landed at a CCS near Swindon at 9 o'clock. I remember my temperature reached 105 and holding out my arm it steamed like a horse after a race. It was good to be washed for the first time for days as I lay with a fearful headache and fits of that helpless shivering which mark the disease. I ate nothing for 3 days. I think they have new medication now, but then I had 3 days of Quinine, 5 days Mepacrine, and 5 days Pernacine (back to bed). Some kind ATS anti-aircraft gunner girls took my clothes and went miles to have them washed and pressed. I noted that my MO was a woman, 'and very pleasant'. In 2003, fifty-nine years later, I noted that my first woman doctor was, 'kind, understanding and very helpful', as, indeed, her successors have continued to be.

It was bliss for that week or two being away from the dirt, the rain – and the danger. But I never got away from that feeling that I was cheating in some way; a pale reflection, I suppose, of the survivor guilt that people felt after Auschwitz. Anyway, I didn't prolong my sick leave unduly, and by 9 August

Normandy revisited, 2002.

I was one of the 1400 crammed into the *Empire Crossbow* – designed for
600 – *en route* for France. There were quite a few first timers, who, I noted,
wore, 'that peculiar expression, a mixture of exasperation at being bitched
about, excitement at the future, refusal to admit any sort of excitement over
anything – all generally to be summed up as a 'I-have-done-all-this-sort-of-
thing-before-but-actually-I-haven't-the-vaguest-idea-what-happens-next'
expression!'

There were also large numbers returning to 51 Div: '...though nobody
from 127 except a new gunner who says he's going to replace Jimmy Mailer
the survey officer – killed while I've been in England.'

Eventually I reached the 36 Reinforcement unit near Bayeux. I began to
harbour hostile feelings towards the base wallahs. I met one: 'He is Mayor
Alcock, once Uncle Arthur in the BBC – a simian poseur ... I was moved to
declaim Sassoon's *Base Details* in its entirety.'

I was determined to get back to 127 – even if it meant upping and leaving
on my own – fortified by the comforting knowledge that the CO had asked
for me by name. I knew that they were having casualties in the break-out
from Normandy. By mid-August I was moved to give a few examples of the

base mentality: 'The sergeant who showed us to our part of the camp, said complacently: "Actually this is my day off but I'm doing this all the same," and the batman who had to get some blankets for us grumbled that he, "was working till half past ten last night fetching and carrying ..." To the Sergeant I said nothing. Such a man who had reached 3 stripes and could yet speak thus, was obviously beyond recall. To the batman I pointed out that half past ten was not usually considered a late hour in a front line unit. This naturally is a resume of my actual speech, which included a few well chosen if not uncommon words.' But by the fifteenth I was back with my Battery near Falaise. We'd had quite a few casualties in the Regiment, particularly FOOs, and there were only seven officers functioning in the Battery. Actually the Regt had had 33% casualties among the officers.

On the 20 August the CO came over to say that Frank was to get a majority and 304 Battery and I was to get F Troop, 304 Battery. I noted that I'd like a third pip but that it did potentially shorten one's life expectation. We continued to advance towards the Seine, sometimes shelled or mortared and on one occasion given a good pounding by 50 Luftwaffe bombers to accompany the shelling from our left flank. After the pouring rain the weather grew warm and sunny as well as wasp and fly-ridden. Once we found a waterfall and enjoyed a cooling shower. One day I wrote: 'It's not often my stomach turns over, but a dead German I saw today was most unpleasant. He'd been hit in the head by a piece of shell, and was covered with flies and wasps. (The same wasps who shared our meals ...) A German horse-drawn battery had also been destroyed. The animals looked awful. Hope to get a chance to write to C this evening, unless (horror) we move again.'

Sometimes we were strafed by FW 190s – a new and formidable German fighter. We were wet, tired, always on the move – usually just when we were about to eat or drink some tea. We neared the Seine, advancing 40-50 miles on 27 August and next day stopped at evening at Bourg-Archard. It was a pleasant experience: 'We advanced again at 10.00 going north to where the Seine does a big loop. We are only 2 or 3 miles from the river. We are in a big farmyard area, and the first troops to have come here. We got a wonderful welcome with flowers and kisses, Calvados, cider, butter, eggs and Bordeaux white wine. I was amazed when I turned up on a motorcycle to be kissed and hugged by all sexes and ages. Tonight they are cooking Bill and me a chicken, and won't accept a bean for it. We, in return, have given cigarettes, matches, chocolate, sweets, soap and various other oddments.'

And writing the next morning I described how:

Slept for 7 blissful hours last night; finished and posted a letter to C this morning. Bill has just come along describing the chicken in terms which make my mouth water. They had laid out all the best china etc, but unfortunately we can't leave the CP which is in a barn. We've fired heavily here – on Germans trying to escape across the river.' It all had to end, of course, and twelve hours later I was describing how at 11.00 hours we, 'went into action at Barneville; but before the guns even got us up, we were off again in the steaming rain, till finally we rendezvoused with the CO2 at a corner where an infantry jeep had just been shot to ribbons by a Spandau. You couldn't go much further than that – the tanks were only a quarter of a mile ahead; and Battalion HQ was in the area. The mortars were behind us. They were still bringing in dead, and wounded about the place, their poor wounds ineffectually covered by stained blankets. Anyway we set in firing vigorously – we've used 1,000 rounds today in the battery – disturbed only by an occasional mortaring on our right.

Jake Mason (D/304) is missing – believed captured, as they've found his carrier but not the crew. It is still raining and very overcast.

21.10: More shells. Vehicles in Waggon Lines hit; no casualties.

21.20: More shells, no casualties.

22.30: Intermittent shelling.'

Jake died of wounds and it was his troop that I was to inherit. On 1 September I joined 304 Battery and met my troop. Next day I was up at 04.00 and: '... meeting the Nos. 1, saying how do you do to the TP etc. It is a good troop I think – bolshie but good in action. A good bit of work remains to be put in on it...Findlay decided to come with me after all, and has met a lot of his friends so *he's* quite happy. We move off very early tomorrow.

21.30: Nearly dark. I am writing by the rising moon. We move at 05.45, and I am still waiting for my Jeep which has gone back for a new carrier... sure enough it was raining and I gulped down my soya link sausage without much enthusiasm, in the rainy darkness, loud with engines revving, cookers roaring and the blasphemous shouts of hurried gunners. However, the Troop was ready on time which rather pleased me, and we began the long march here. The march here was quite memorable. We had a tremendous welcome in Rouen (whose cathedral is *lovely*) and the column showered cigarettes, biscuits etc all along the route. Coming up towards the coast, people were weeping and laughing with joy. Looking at them, it was impossible to believe our coming here has brought them anything but happiness.

I described the carrier crew I'd got together: 'The driver is first class but I may lose him through nose trouble. The Ack (Butcher) is quite new to the job, but intelligent, speaks French, sketches etc and for want of a better expression, is a gentleman. Shows signs of becoming a first class scrounger. This is his first campaign, but John Clark, my GPO (same applies) says he's good under fire. The two signallers – Allen and Horton. Allen is goodish, Horton fair. I could do worse, also much better. In the TP, the BSM is a weak link, the Nos. 1 are, I think patchy, but I like the troop.' My Ack – Charles Butcher, later Sergeant, MM became a friend whom I sought in vain after the war. So I was delighted to get his letter in 2006 telling me he'd loved *Field of Fire* which he spotted in the local library, then traced me through the internet and wrote suggesting a meeting. Sure enough, he came to lunch – elderly but very much the same person and we swapped our post-war life stories. 'We all knew about The Diary', he told me, 'and as you lay on your stretcher, you gasped "My Diary, my basin" and we put them with you'. Alas, his oral cancer has limited recent contact.

I noted that I'd be supporting the Black Watch and that: 'Mess conversation is along the "it's been nice knowing you" lines so I am (in spite of myself) somewhat depressed. I wish I could see C again, which is silly because it would only make things harder. Damn the Germans and roll on peace!'

Now that I'm old and soft and cross if my bedroom radiator isn't hot in the morning, I look back in my diary and am amazed at the hardship we overcame. Of course we were young but even so .... Take 8 September 1944 for example, on which I wrote:

I want to write up yesterday fully, so that in days to come if I am ever tempted to say of all this, 'It wasn't so bad', I have at least one reminder of an occasion when it bloody well was so bad!

The day really started on the evening of the 6th, when after hanging about for hours waiting for instructions, I was told that owing to an RAF programme, I should not man the OP at first light, but no sooner had I returned to the carrier than I was told we had to be ready at 06.30. OK. I warned the crew and the guard and went to bed. It was raining and some was dripping in so I turned my bed around. At 02.40 hours there was a sudden awful gush of water and about 3 gallons of it poured into my trench. The cover had collapsed. The trench was quite soon 9 inches deep in water. The next half hour was a true nightmare. Somehow I got dressed into wet clothes, got my bedding into the soaking Jeep (it was still raining hard) and huddled into the front of a 15 cwt wrapped into wet blankets till 06.00. At 06.30 we set off for the OP still in the pelting rain, and eventually after scrounging a little breakfast from the infantry manned it about 08.30 with an infantry platoon as local protection. Prior to this I went up with the BC before daylight proper. By then I was of course quite drenched. We had to leave the carrier about ½ a mile back and carry phones, remote control etc up to the OP. The OP was in an orchard and gave a good view of the Boche defences round Octerike which are very numerous and formidable. I need hardly say that to crown everything the local weather and one thing and another made communications almost impossible, as the phones kept breaking down and something was wrong with the wireless. At 15.00 we returned for an RAF bombing which never took place (still raining furiously) and after a cup of tea went out with the relief platoon about 17.30. We also had a tin of M & V which tasted unusually good. Well, it went on raining till near darkness (Alistair C. came up to the same place to man the 126 OP) so we went in. We were mortared twice by our own mortars and shelled once by our own guns but otherwise it was a quiet enough day. We knocked off 3 chickens and 2 lbs of sugar from a deserted farm. When I got back Findlay had dried by blankets and sleeping bag, put me out a clean pillow case and made up my bed in a loft (my new safari camp bed arrived from the Hornsfield people of Croydon on the 6th) and at 23.00 after a wonderful cup of tea, and issue of rum, I took off all my wet things and fell straight asleep – god how good it was – and the last sound I heard was the rain beating on the roof.

This was just before my first time as FOO with the 5th Black Watch. There was to be a big attack on Le Havre and, frankly, I was rather scared – not only of the obvious but also of not doing my job well. In the event, I did become rather an efficient gunner and one of my proudest moments was when the company commander I was to support in a coming attack, greeted me with 'Oh good, I hoped it would be you.'

I described the battle for Le Havre as something of a walkover, which indeed it was, though there was one alarming episode, when: 'We had a Sherman with us, pumping away at a pillbox nearby, and suddenly as darkness began to fall, the rumble of treads was heard ahead of us. "Christ!", said the Tank Commander and began to back away, "It's the Tigers". I was in the middle of the road when the first stream of tracer bullets shot past. I flattened out and managed to crawl into the nearby orchard and put through a call to the BC on the blower for a couple of tanks. The bullets flew for about 20 minutes before somebody discovered it was one of our own. Shermans shooting us up!'

The place was full of concrete strong points from which we all gathered the loot which was the FOO's compensation for being in harm's way: watches, Lugers, binoculars, booze, and in this instance, a useful pair of *donkey's ears*

– a periscope which you could put over the parapet instead of your own head. I collected a watch and a cut throat razor for Findlay. After the action there was a long letter from Clare – something which kept me going over the difficult months ahead. Such letters were sometimes described as 'five minutes leave'.

Late in September we reached Calais. In the sunlight I could see the white cliffs of Dover. All along what the Germans presumably expected to be the invasion coast were defences of every kind and anti-airborne poles on a scale no-one dreamed of in England. How lucky we chose Normandy, I thought. I suppose it was being so close to home that filled me with gloomy thoughts of the past five years. Anyway, I ended my diary entry for the 23rd: 'What a world it is; I am sad and homesick tonight on the shores of Calais.'

A few days later, I watched a huge raid by the RAF heavies which I described as 'terrifying'. I added: 'But the worst thing I saw was when a Lancaster, flying very slowly and low down, must have had its pilot hit for quite suddenly it turned over and plummeted nose down into the earth, bursting into violent red flame as it struck. Nobody in it could have had a chance, and yet they must have had eight or nine seconds in the certainty of death. And as they burned with their plane, still more of those bombs struck all around where they lay, till the flaming pyre was hidden too. I felt rather sick. And yet – one could hardly believe it – by afternoon those damned guns were firing again. Letter from C this morning. I sent two off to her. Meant to write tonight, but we moved and now I have a big headache so I'm going to sleep.'

It was beginning to dawn on us (as it must have to the Wehrmacht in 1941) that we were in for a much unwanted winter campaign and so it turned out as we moved through Belgium, where one day:

We did 189 miles, starting at 06.30 and arriving at 21.00. We seemed to pass through history yesterday; right through the Ypres – all the old historical names – Sanctuary Wood, Paschendale, Mount Kemmel. We went through the huge Menin gate carved with its thousands of names.

My sons took me back there in 2003 and I have a photograph of me taken among the pillars. Strangely, I thought it was my first visit and had no recall of 1944. I manned a series of rather sinister OPs in the woods of Holland: places where vision was restricted and a Sten gun a useful item because of enemy snipers and raiding patrols. For the first time I couldn't risk bringing my Diary with me and left it in the gun line. Early in October, I did a long

60-hour OP stint. One grew jumpy. I tried to describe this in my entry for 4 October. Here is part of it:

> a.m. OP: It is difficult to convey a good picture of night in the front line. It grows – it seems – suddenly quite dark – and every bush – so innocent by day – seems to hold an enemy sniper – every shell which lands seems to be enemy. Last night the Gordons started firing everything off on our left, by way of a demonstration and it brought back a decent measure of retaliation by way of mortar and shellfire from the Boche. However, I see that sentence means nothing unless you were here. It doesn't begin to give you that feeling in the stomach as you hear the fantastically loud rattle of machine guns, and the splintering crash of mortars, or the sudden approaching scream of a shell – and you know it's close and you say as nonchalantly as you can, 'Down boys!' and down you all go and the damn thing crashes just in front of you and the splinters come hurtling through the trees like steel rain. And you pick yourself up and say to the Company Commander as casually as you can, 'Hm, fairly close ...' and hope he won't notice the slight unsteadiness in your voice, but when he answers, his voice is unsteady too so you feel better about it all. It is never silent for long up here in the woods at night. Nervous triggers make every short silence end suddenly – and indeed the sound of bullet is almost less worrying than silence. I am with the same Coy. here as at Havre and a damn nice lot they are.

I was poorly: colds, coughs and a foot, infected in the desert, giving trouble. At the end of October I was in a dawn attack in Holland. I was with the leading companies and narrowly survived Spandau fire at my carrier; mortaring and shellfire and a big splinter missed my ankle by less than six inches. I'd always been horrified by any cruelty to animals, and here I had to record two traumatic events:

> The tanks started numerous fires with their big guns, and a sight which sickened me was some cows screaming and trying to escape from a flaming barn, as they burnt to death alive – flames from nose to tail. Awful, and one could do nothing. Mercifully the barn fell quickly in and ended it. (We had an excellent breakfast cooked on one of these flaming barns.) ... Shot a wounded horse with my Sten. Both front legs broken and it wouldn't stay still, but my first shot right in its forehead put it out of pain for ever.

The December 2005 issue of *Military Illustrated* featured extracts from *Field of Fire* from that October to late November as we advanced through

Holland to the river Maas. People didn't always realise – indeed I myself didn't at first – how many details attended preparation for battle. 'Teed up' as I described it on 21 October:

> Wireless sets checked, batteries filled, maps marked, chinagraphs sharpened, bootlaces tested, Stens and revolvers cleaned, rations, petrol and water loaded, binoculars cleaned, compasses tested, vehicles checked, cable checked – these are only a few of the larger and more important things one has to do before going forward with an attack. I alone have 3 wireless sets – a No. 22 to communicate with BC and guns, a No. 18 to talk to the infantry, and a No. 38 if my remote control cable from me to my wireless in the carrier, is destroyed.

These weeks were wet, cold, dirty and dangerous. However, many of the farmers had fled and there was livestock to be shot – and eaten. I was able to exchange hospitality with Sandy Leslie, whose Black Watch company I often supported. The menu sometimes included roast chicken, duckling and roast suckling pig, prepared by my villainous Irish cook, Paddy Gavigan. Usually I wrote that it was cold and raining or that we had heavy frost or snow. It was difficult to find good OPs; it could involve a couple of ladders propped up to the roof of a derelict farmhouse. Indeed, it was on such an occasion that my OP was described by the war correspondent Chester Wilmot who later became well known. I have his book *The Struggle for Europe* on my bookshelf. This, however, was a small encounter. About sixty years later I was at a dinner party, when a fellow guest from the BBC was asking me about the war and suggested I contact their archive department to see if there were any record of the occasion. There was, indeed, a tape which had been broadcast on the BBC's nightly *War Report*. I was able to obtain a copy which I have played to the young officers at Larkhill to whom I am invited to talk from time to time. We all enjoy the bangs and crashes and Mr Wilmot.

My experience of the fighting that winter is encapsulated in a Diary entry dated 18 November. I'd like to include it in full:

> Night: Called out yesterday in the pouring rain just before evening meal, and arrived soaked at Bn. HQ to find I was FOO for yet another canal assault that night. Hell, how it rained and how cold it was in the artificial moonlight waiting for the flails to finish beating the track forward to B. Coy. I got there eventually, walking ahead of my carrier and spent the night in heavy shelling. We had about 100 in the first hour, most of them very close – one seven yards

from the carrier, which cut the wireless lead. Trees were sawn in half by the vicious, slashing splinters and the pieces of warm steel tinkled down, mingling with the rain. We were cold, tired and hungry. When we advanced to the canal bank my carrier got bogged, so did the tank I got hold of to fish it out. Eventually a half track did the job, but as we did the last open stretch to the canal (I was still on foot) we got caught in a rain of about 50 shells which were so close one *had* to lie down and wait and hope for the best as they screamed towards you and crashed – some sending the lethal fragments whizzing only inches overhead as you pressed close to the soft earth, tin hat close to the floor, body straining to press lower, nerves shrinking, hope fading ... Several times in those few minutes I thought 'this one is it, this time it'll hit me.' But we crossed in our assault boat. We had to leave the carrier and carry our wireless and necessaries (no food) on helped by a party of Jocks. Got to Bn. HQ in time for another plastering and found the BC half dead with fatigue, on the wireless. Then marched on to B. Coy. and established an OP about dawn. Cold but no rain. During the morning word came that the Bn was pulling out in the afternoon, and our party returned in the sunshine. Coming back over the sunny, green pinewoods and grass near the canal, it was hard to re-visualise the hours of fear in the darkness, when each hundred yards seemed a mile, and the newly dead turned their waxen faces to the unreal moon, and the wounded sobbed as the stretcher-bearers plodded back with them through the mud. War is not pretty, and though I am used enough to dead men by now, it always seems such a waste to see them lying there cold and white and gone so far away. Can't we find a better answer to life than this? I hope my son, if ever I have one, won't have to do the things I've done; before I knew I used to think it was 'exciting' this thing they called battle, but it isn't, it's achingly tiring, and heartbreaking. No sleep of course last night and I'm going to sleep the clock round now. Letters from George Long and Clare. Must try to write to her tomorrow. Spent all last night drenched to the skin, what a luxury to take off wet socks today and bathe one's tired feet and have a wash.

I became tired and despondent: 'But on a day like this it is quite impossible to visualise surviving this bloody war. Perhaps the very will to live is sapped by the endless rain and the soul destroying mud.'

How did they survive in 1917? Between Nijmegen and the Rhine I relieved some US paratroops, scruffy but generous, and scrounged much excellent food, including a *3 pound* tin of coffee (all later stolen from my carrier). It was our first experience of shumines, devilish little wooden devices which removed a foot or a leg – logistically more effective than a killing.

By December, I was describing, 'days of flap and frayed tempers'. The fighting had died down and I went on leave to Antwerp where I had a couple of lucky escapes. The first was when I was out and a V1 hit part of my hotel and covered my bed with flying glass. Then on the twentieth I was going to see Gary Cooper in the Plainsman at the Rex Cinema. As it happened, I got the timing wrong, had to give it a miss and went shopping just round the corner. There was a loud explosion and the shop windows collapsed. The Rex had been hit by a V2 with 900 killed including troops on leave – which was immediately cancelled. My Battery Sergeant Major – due for UK leave – was killed. News started coming in about a serious German offensive in Belgium.

Christmas Day ... ah yes; let me quote:

Noon: The worst ever. We are waiting to move! Back into Belgium where the enemy is apparently penetrating around Liège. The situation is in fact pretty serious, but even on top of a hangover from last night, morale is good all round. We had Xmas dinner, a tree, and everything laid on but all that has had to be scrapped now, though we are doing our best to get the meal out by Troops. At first one couldn't believe it as we'd almost been guaranteed Xmas. Still, it's no use grumbling. Heavy frost, sunshine, and bitter cold today. 2 letters from C last night which cheered me up a lot – also we had a good booze up and I am (almost cheerfully) resigned to whatever may happen now.

20.30, south of Liege – Strivay: Drive of 40 miles in icy weather. Tremendous welcome in Liège where we were the first British column ever into the city. We are going to have an Xmas dinner soon.' We did. On 29th Arnhem radio reported: 'The most dangerous German thrust to the Meuse has been blunted and thrown back 3 miles by the crack British 51st Division, famed since the African Campaign and veterans of the Normandy battles..' I reacted: 'This is distinctly news to us; thank the Lord it's not true!'

Days followed conventionally: orders, counter orders, confusion in fearful cold and blinding snowstorms; this sort of thing:

1300, Warizy: Nightmare day yesterday. We set out at 08.00 and eventually after much ditching, sliding and cursing reached our mountainous OP. The snow was knee deep but at first visibility was clear and we had a fine view. Later it began to snow, and we got wireless orders that the plan of attack had been changed and we were to come down and make for here. It took

La Roche-en-Ardenne, 1945.

us a good time to do this, but we did finally reach Verdenne, the start point
– full of knocked out Panther tanks and a few bodies, and at this point my
wireless went dis. The main axis was not a road at all; it was a path bulldozed
through the hills and valleys, full of snow and ice. On the right a few German
tanks threw high velocity shells about the place....Took 40 minutes to get more
water and by then night had fallen though the artificial moonlight cast a glow
over the snowy wilderness and dark patches of Christmas trees. We pushed
on; twice we got ditched, and twenty times nearly ditched. I was driving (the
Jeep) and had Butcher and Allen with me. We still hadn't eaten or brewed since
07.30.

On 14 January I was supporting A company beyond La Roche. It was
snowing and *very* cold. Here are a few excerpts from what followed:

Ronnie and I were in Jeep OPs .... during the afternoon we ran up against a
detachment of 2 Panther tanks, 140 men and Spandaus and a 2 in. mortar
team. Some panic as our own tanks were held up further back ... The 3 tanks
who came up headed by my Jeep were not a success. One had a jammed gun
and engine failure; another was brewed up, and the third could not get to us.
All this time we were getting a pleasant reception from over the way. I managed

to get some orders back lying under my jeep with AP shells whizzing over the top and a few bursts of m.g. fire. Very unpleasant. I got in some shelling, both 25 pds and medium, which seemed to quieten things down. We had about 7 wounded, and one chap we had to leave out wounded, died. So there we were pinned down and B Coy. went round. Nothing to eat since 06.00 and we got nothing till next 03.00. It was bitterly cold – 32 degrees of frost, and some people collapsed. Everybody's feet were agony and our teeth chattered and we shivered violently in the bitter cold. Not a building in sight. About 05.30 we reached the farm area which had been holding us up and advanced again soon after dawn.... we met the tanks again in the village on the ridge beyond. They knocked out one of our SPs (killing 3 and wounding one) and three or four Shermans which blazed in the snow. From the left flank two more tanks – one a Tiger – shelled us incessantly. There were more casualties, and Bill Fraser, the Pioneer officer, was killed by a splinter in the belly. My OP was (and is) in the attic of a small house. Excellent view. Eventually I found the Panthers and got a medium Regt on them – or rather on one of them. Got some extremely close rounds – one seemed almost a direct hit, and the tank scurried away.

This, I think, has been the hardest battle I've ever seen, conditions being appalling. Had my first wash and shave for 3 days today and was horrified by my face in the mirror!'

Next day: 'Rested yesterday and went with the CO to where I shelled my tank. Found about a dozen rounds within 100 yards, and one actually 4 yards away. Very pleasing – the CO tickled pink ... Everybody in great form as they always are after a successful action – and there's no doubt the Div has acquired considerable merit by this latest attack. I shan't forget for a long time the red blood on the white snow, and the tanks splattered with blood where the AP shot had riddled them. Or the night of agonising cold and fear with the battle loud and angry on all sides as "ignorant armies clashed by night" – the numbness and pain of the feet, the drenching tiredness, the twinges of fear, and the night sky lit by flashes, and the whistle of shells nearby as one crouched in the snowy ditch, soaked, and tired beyond belief.

How rotten the way January ended. I was racked with toothache and my little dog, Happy, got cancer and had to be shot. I've never had another dog; lots of cats including Bella, my little tabby stray, companion of my old age.

Early in February and beset by headaches, I started to prepare for my part in Operation 'Veritable'. In due course I found myself supporting A Company at night in the Reichswald forest. Pandemonium. Above, the excellently helpful 'artificial moonlight' all around, the skyline aflame with

John Stevenson.

gun flashes. Somewhere the haunting music of the bagpipes mingled with the whizzing bullets. I had some good shooting but we suffered numerous casualties. In Gennep after the battle I was able to report: 'Tonight – over 110 hours since I put them on – I am about to remove my boots and socks from my tired feet. I shall also undress. The Spandau fire which has made the last two days hideous has died down now as our advance pushed southwards, and it is silent in rainy, ruined Gennep except for the occasional crash of an enemy shell – and there are some big ones coming over – evidently from heavy guns in the Siegfried Line.'

'Damn and blast and bloody everything,' I wrote on 20 January (remarkably mildly), back in Holland once again and miserable with toothache and departed dog. Steve – John Stevenson the GPO of my Troop – and I spent time again with the Troupin family – fast becoming friends. We'd already met the children (of which there were five) sometime before. 'They are', I wrote, 'actually small fiends in human guise and rush shrieking about the house all day long in noisy clogs.' There was heavy snow, but on the last day of January:

Worse perhaps even than the numbing snow, now comes the rain – slashing down and turning the snow carpet into muddy brown and green fields. Driving on the roads last night was damn dangerous as they were nothing but sheet ice and the car shot all over the road as soon as one touched the accelerator let alone the brakes.

A murderous, abscessed tooth was removed with heavenly relief but, of course, long-term implications. By now we were being briefed about a large forthcoming operation. 'Veritable – even bigger than Alamein', and supported by 1,000 guns. Clearly, previous experience was beginning to take its toll because – like most soldiers, I suppose:

> In a way I shall be glad when it does start, for though battle is fearful and full of its own sort of terror, it is worse to lie in bed 2 nights – and then one night – before; thinking of the awful wounds we may get, of the hideous crashing of enemy shells and mortars, the singing bullets – and ahead in the darkness the hostile darkness and the enemy – and the ground teeming with every sort of devilish mine. And you lie there sweating, your brain ticking over feverishly and you just can't sleep and you think oh God let it start, then at least it will finish ... However, once in battle I am not particularly worried by such things. The danger is tangible. One crouches cringing from splinters and bullets – but there it is – if you're hit you're hit and you never think you will be anyway. Funny how you don't.

At 03.00 we started to move up towards our start point, one and a half hours late, of course, and I, with 'an awful headache' supervising the camouflage. I found time to send Clare letter twenty-four. I had a new battery commander by now: 'Bill French, a "floating" major from 59 Agra who came to the Regt recently as a replacement for such occasions, is coming to us. He's a very nice chap – I went with him to that VT fuse lecture the other day. He's now commanded both the other batteries and been 2nd i/c as well, so he should be getting to know the Regt pretty well.' He'd reached a stage where I wrote before 'Veritable': '...Bill French, our acting BC is a very nice chap and most easy to get on with.'

On 7 February I left my customary pre-battle – potentially valedictory! – message for Clare. I see that, as I survived, it was 'duly rubbed out' on 20 February. I've already given you a brief portrait of the opening of 'Veritable' in the Reichswald Forest. We broke out of it and took our objectives. By morning, ordered to establish an OP near the Gennep road, which we intended to cut, I emerged at the wheel of my (now brakeless) Jeep over a heavily mortared bridge up over a mile onwards, angrily machine gunned from my right flank. Bullets flew over us, behind us and before us, bouncing off the road. I drove flat out, weaving from side to side wild with what? Fear? Exhilaration? Perhaps determination. Anyway I reached my OP – a church tower I persuaded the PIAT gunners to spare – and spent many testing hours there. I put down the only – and very effective – smoke screen of my army career. (Proud to say that it is mentioned – without accreditation – on page 216 of the Highland Division history!) At one stage, I saw the unwelcome sight of many square helmets gleaming in the sun; presumably a counter-attack which I set about discouraging with some accurate shellfire. None of the 'Troop Target Fireplan' so beloved of my OCTU instructors. No, it was 'Mike bloody target' straight away – using all twenty-four of my regiment's guns. At 16.00 we had some bacon – our first food since tea, bread and jam early in the day. At dark, I left the icy, windswept tower and joined Sandy Leslie in a cellar until relieved by Bill French at 22.00. Then 'some good, broken sleep'. A few days later, I was snug in Gennep in a warm cellar on a thick mattress, numbed by the harmless (to me) shells falling in the streets above. Indeed I rejoiced in a rubber hot water bottle I'd found. A bit soon; a nasty surprise awaited me next day.

14 February 09.50, 6 (Can) General Hospital, Vucht:

At about 16.00 on 13 Feb – 2 years to the day since Jock was killed – I was wounded. My whole crew and I were packing the carrier in the street as I'd decided to send my jeep back for an overhaul, and there'd been quite a lot of shelling nearby. All of a sudden (and I didn't even hear it coming) there was a blinding flash the other side of the road and I felt a sharp pain (no it was really hardly a pain so much as the stab you get from an injection) in my right leg, and down I went. The others, all except Shepherd, were in the cellar, but Shepherd fell in the road with about 8 wounds. I got the others up and we hauled him in and shell dressed him, and I gave him a shot of morphia. One of his fingers was hanging off, he was hit in both legs – one broken below the knee, neck and back. Turning to my own leg I was rather shaken to find the blood was not oozing but squirting, a small artery having been hit, but Steve quickly got a homemade tourniquet onto it and the bleeding died down. Then they got us on stretchers to the 5 Bn RAP nearby where the MO gave me some morphia too and so we travelled back through the night in jolting ambulances along the bumpy roads round Nijmegen till, in the middle of the night, we got here. Much devotion by Shepherd who begged all the doctors to be allowed to stay with me and embarrassed me a lot by saying publicly how he'd never forget how I'd treated him first! I'm not altogether sorry to get a short rest as I was getting tired – and 5½ months was a good run as FOO without a scratch. However, I expect I'll be back soon.

The hospital train – narrowly missed by a V1 ('Get the fuck out of here' suggested the wounded) – took seven long hours to Brussels. I'm a bit ashamed to admit that, as soon as I realised that my wound wasn't serious, I felt intense relief that I'd be out of harm's way for a while; clearly not for very long, I realised in Brussels. And, well before my next birthday, I was back with my battery; and booked for FOO for our next job – crossing the Rhine.

Two notable reunions took place in Brussels. On 19 February:

> To my delight, today (in response to a note I'd sent him) in rolled old Roden Parry, my best friend for years and one I've only seen once since the war. He is now a major RA at Rear HQ 21 AG and hasn't changed at all. He told me his father died at the end of December as well as 2 of his 3 brothers killed in action. Also that George Russ, the third member of our trio known as the Old Firm at school, works just near him and will also come and see me. He's also buying me some clothes from the officers shop.

Also, I had lunch with George Baker – a former – and well liked CO – 'resplendent as a full Colonel, but wishing he was back with the Regiment'. I can't exactly recall how it arose, but there was some thought that I might join his staff, because, I wrote: 'I'm really beginning to wonder how much more front line I can stand, and yet each time I think of it I feel I should be betraying something – myself and my friends (Jock perhaps) and everything I admire, and so I suppose I shall steam off back and get wounded again, or killed or just by some stroke of luck survive completely. I do so hate these base-wallahs – not the genuine ones, but the stacks of cowards and incompetents who hide down here and let others do the work. I don't think I could be happy with such people after over 2 years in my Regiment. So there it is. I wish I were a bit more of a realist and I've no doubt I'd get myself some sort of quite interesting job down here and be done with it. But I don't think I am, so I must start steeling myself mentally for a return to the mud and general bloodiness of a troop commander's lot.' George became a Field Marshal and Master Gunner. At Larkhill, Home of the Royal Regiment of Artillery, Pete and I were shown the enormous display case containing all his honours and decorations.

With thoughts of return to 304, I had to start getting my kit together. I encountered some problems:

No news today except that I got some kit at the QM below the hospital. Also Roden called with some more clothes – very nice of him to bother. Yet when I suggested that it was maybe too much trouble to come daily, he just said, 'What – for you?' and left it at that. I felt quite humble ... Got one of the local ward-women to wash my clothes today. Rather annoyingly the leg of my only pair of pants is soaked in blood, and my right boot is also heavily caked. Even the sole is deeply stained. Also my sheepskin has bloodstains all over it – I suppose from when I lay on the floor after fixing Shepherd up and when I was beginning to black out a bit. Anyway there's more blood about than I thought. Also I've lost 3 out of 4 socks and 1 garter! Still, Roden brought me 2 damn good new pairs. Sent C no. 30.

Early in March, something happened which I should really have included in some short stories I wrote in Germany:

Then I went around trying to do some shopping, but I could not find what I wanted. Eventually I dropped into a bar quite aimlessly and got pretty sozzled. Quite an attractive girl came in and sat with me (a hostess or something) and gradually got extremely amorous and begged me to sleep with her, gave me her address, declared she 'loffed' me etc etc. She passed out after about 4 hours steady drinking and I walked a little unsteadily out, found a tram and got back here and fell into bed, spending all yesterday with a rather severe hangover. Rather a curious little adventure really. I've heard of such thing happening but they don't often happen to me! I must say I was vaguely embarrassed when the girl started tearing off portions of clothing, but I maintained a dead pan and assured myself mentally that this was the continent etc etc! Anyway no harm done.

The early days of March were, in fact, a pleasant round of shopping, bridge, much drinking and letters and cigarettes from home. I see that I met a couple of press blokes: '..throwing back whisky fast and I had half a dozen on their expenses sheet. We leave here tomorrow and shall spend a night in 's Hertogenbosch. Lovely bath. Now for lovely sleep. Sent C no, 41 last night.'

I got back to the Regiment on 10 March, found a Black Watch friend, Major Alec Brodie, had performed heroic deeds and been recommended for the VC but 'only' got a DSO. Alec had a shark-like mouth in a ferocious face. Our POWs were always sure he would execute them, although out of combat he was a real pussy cat.

Apparently I'd been put up for an MC (second time) but no luck. I had to wait for it until hostilities had ceased and I was Adjutant in 1945. We had a new CO – with an MC – ex anti-tank (not *real* gunners we always said). Our BC was posted to Larkhill and I wrote: 'This means that though we lose one good BC, we shall get Bill French in his place, who will also undoubtedly be absolutely first class.' Bill had, indeed, won golden opinions in the Ardennes and the Reichswald. At Ronnie's boozy departure party he confided that D Troop, when I took it over, was regarded as the worst in the Regiment and C the best. D was now regarded as better than C. I felt proud.

Once again the scores of jobs preceding a large attack; the troubled nights, the message ('Duly deleted') for Clare and, after crossing the glassy Rhine in the first shimmer of the dawn of 24 March, a seriously unfriendly reception. For example:

(As I wrote the last sentence a mortar bomb landed within 25 yards showering dirt all over me, so I've moved into the carrier, which is a safer spot.) Moaning minnies and Spandau bullets have also been in evidence all day. Stuff is now once more falling damn close all around. Another of the day's incidents was when Bill Bradford decided to hold an O Gp at about 5 and a mortar bomb landed slap next door to Bn HQ, setting it and the adjoining farm on very vigorous fire. The Boche then mortared and shelled the fire for about an hour while we held an improvised O Gp in a house a few doors away. Rees, which we can see very clearly about a mile away, looks ruined and is on fire in many places.

And a couple of days later:

Went on shooting hard all day as plenty of targets cropped up. The weather was still fine. I was damnably tired and my lips were cracked and sore from the dust and the wind. The OP was a ruined attic which presented a good view. Almost everywhere the countryside was in flames with great smoke pyres rising skywards – including on our lines. Before this attack started, J ---- As I started that sentence, four shells landed plumb outside this HQ with 4 sudden crashes – 2 wounded, one pretty badly – I was going to write Jerry gave us a most savage pasting with mortars and AP shot. He got 3 almost direct hits on us and the roof came tumbling in. Same thing most of yesterday with a lot of rifle and machine gun sniping. The enemy was very close all round the posn,

The author and Kondor, 1946.

and in the afternoon the tanks with a platoon of B Coy, blasted and winkled them out, collecting about 50 prisoners. Came down to B Coy HQ and had 8 ½ hours' sleep and it was welcome!

By the 28th I was weary, deadly tired. I wrote: 'I've not had my clothes off since the attack started, which counting D-1 is 6 days by the end of tonight.' We moved eastward with sporadic fighting during April; typified on the sixth for example: 'We shoved on up the road till we came to a small blown bridge where the fun started. We were mortared, shelled and machine-gunned. Had 6 casualties. There were also AP mines. I walked on with the Coy with a 38 set working to the carrier and I got some good shooting – about 250 rounds in all after which the enemy shut up and retired, followed by the 5/7 Gordons who came through us.'

I remember, during the street fighting, entering a basement, tin-hatted, pistol in hand and finding it full of old men, women and children who glared at me with fear and hatred. I felt a sort of shame but – unlike the SS

– molested no-one; and within weeks the troops were giving their sweets and chocolates to these same children.

So we continued onwards in April. The countryside was lovely, I wrote: '... almond and cherry trees in their first blossoming already dusty from the convoys, the trees budding', and, I added: 'How lovely England would be looking now ... the bluebells in the woods and the quiet villages and little streams, and the swallows coming back and "hearts at peace under an English heaven"...'

I was due for leave in May and that – and the realisation that the war might be nearly over – led to a feeling of caution. 'Each day', I wrote, 'leave grows nearer and each day it seems to grow further away. The thought of going into battle grows more repugnant as the time for going to England grows close.'

We approached Bremen and Hamburg which might prove unpleasant, as did Bremervoerde where, at the beginning of May, I nearly joined a couple of people killed in a shower of 88 mm airburst and Moaning Minnies. By then I had been listed LOB (left out of battle) – the battle that was expected. But by 4 May the war ended and I was able to write: 'It seems strange to think that I may (repeat MAY) never have to risk my life in battle again.'

And so, the day the war in Europe ended – VE Day, 8 May (and two years later my wedding day) – I left Calais soon after noon. The day before, my train had trundled through Holland and Belgium greeted by cheers and V signs and, in Holland, a mass of orange flags. I reached Calais at 03.30 and dropped into a bed somewhere until 8 o'clock. I noted in my diary: 'Last time I saw Calais was when we attacked it last year, and I remember standing on the obstacle-studded beach near Gris Nez and seeing the white cliffs in the sunshine – so near it seemed and yet how many dangerous weeks have gone by before – today – I can look on them again.'

I reached a London filled with rejoicing revellers but felt only what these days Bill French and I recall as immense relief and tiredness. Chatting in Wimbledon, we two old men now find it hard to visualise the life we took in our stride over sixty years ago. On VE Day I felt anti- climax and depression. I wrote this sonnet. It isn't very good but it was how I felt.

> O go not, Victory, amid the throng
> Of merrymakers; that is not your place,
> You are not merry, for the war was long,
> And tears they shed not, often stained your face.
> No, rather walk among the ancient dead

Who waited silent with you since the day
When, far from home, they bled their lives away –
They waited for you; go to them instead
And tell them as they rest there in the rain
In all the lonely places where they lie
That, eased by them, we'll not forget their pain,
Nor break the faith that they would not deny,
Now that we find some loveliness again
Because, through them, our laughter did not die.

The year in occupied Germany, that was to pass before I was demobbed – on 1 May 1946 – was, basically, pleasurable. Swimming in hot summer in the river Aller, galloping my spirited bay horse Kondor in the misty dawns, Courts Martial of unfortunate DPs (Displaced Persons) seeking (understandable) revenge. And – to the surprise of all – especially myself – appointed Adjutant.

We had Highland Games. There was much drinking. Non-Fraternising – largely ignored – was finally dropped and an ample sex life enjoyed with the attractive locals; some of whom returned to the UK with a wedding ring. I had plenty of time to write to Clare. My diary ended on 21 August and the day before, I sent her No. 157. She had probably equalled that; not to mention the parcels, clothes and other necessities. It's time to fast forward nearly a year to 1946.

CHAPTER 7

1946-52. 'CIVVIE STREET' AND ADVERTISING. ZENA

It is the spring of 1946 and of the two most important women of my life, one is about to enter it and the other is facing a long departure. I had first met 'Clare' (except fleetingly in 1941) in January 1943. I had returned from North Africa where her husband, Jock Cochrane, had been killed. I had written, said I hoped we might meet and phoned on my return. We met in London. She went home and told her mother she had made a friend for life. When I saw her to the train, I said 'Shall I see you again?' In the spring of 1945 as we prepared for D-Day, Clare and I became very close. Emotion was near the surface in wartime when you couldn't count on a future. We had exchanged nearly 200 letters while I was in Europe. We didn't keep them, and 60 years later couldn't think what on earth we'd written; apart from the obvious. I looked on her small daughter as one of my own; and still regard Jane (now a grandmother herself) as my stepdaughter. Just as Clare sees my elder son Richard as the son she didn't have. I did indeed turn out to be that friend for life. And life reunited us in an unexpected way. On my seventieth birthday I received a letter from Jane, reminding me – as if it were necessary – who she was, and telling me that as she was going to Libya in search of her father's grave, her mother had suggested contacting me for background and possible advice. I phoned immediately and she and her nice Greek husband came to supper the next day. Rapport was immediate and complete; and has remained so for another twenty-two years. She wrote me long letters about her life and I gave her some written items about mine. Clare and I thus rediscovered forgotten years. Then in 1990 Clare's second husband died. Zena, my late wife-to-be, went on her annual trip to Canada, and with her permission I wrote to Clare and we met again, and over the years in due course my family were invited to Jane's large London house for lunch and became friends not only with her children but also with *their* children. How little I could have visualised all that as I spent the day of Jane's birthday in Benghazi on the last day of 1942.

'Clare' and her daughter.

Our two families spent time together. Zena and Clare didn't meet, but accepted and respected each other; and Clare and I eventually agreed that we'd each been wise marrying someone else. However, all that was unknown when in May 1946 I was demobbed and about to look for a job.

After the certainty of uniform I found my 'civvies' really distasteful – especially the awful shoes – so pointed and uncomfortable after nearly seven years of army boots. And of course, I missed the planned regularity of army life which during the summer of 1945 had been so pleasantly improved with swimming and riding my horse Kondor. With my friend Neil, I'd gallop across the plain and through the forest before breakfast or trek out to a German inn for beer and sandwiches on high summer mornings. Neil was another friend lost to cancer before the millennium.

What to do for a living? I could have had my old job back but I had turned my back on journalism and didn't see myself as a reporter. Somebody – I can't remember who – said what about advertising? I didn't actually know anything about it, or what it would entail for me. I think I had some vague idea about writing slogans. Anyway, I went to see a couple of Advertising Agency bosses and was offered two jobs in one day. One of them was in 'the media department' which didn't sound very exciting. The other .... I was interviewed by the American boss as he lay in his bath. Would I fetch him some coffee? I would. I was employed somewhat vaguely and it turned out that as well as writing a few ads I was a sort of 'gopher': chauffeur of his large American car (to collect his glamorous Swedish mistress), organising phones for the office using US nylons as bribes, operating the switchboard and more or less anything else. My adjutant skills were usefully employed! One day my boss Pat Dolan, by now well-known (possibly notorious) in London media circles, said to me, 'Jack, you're now an account executive'. I still thought that meant something to do with invoices, and wasn't attracted. Of course I learned better – and other aspects of the business – specially the seamy side – quite rapidly. In due course I became a copywriter, which was well suited to my abilities, and then Overseas Manager, which entailed travel to many countries over the years.

August 1946. I am in UNRRA the UN refugees organisation, when, moving briskly ahead of me a most elegant bottom belonging to Zena, my wife-to-be and my companion for sixty-three more years. Denis Carter's wife Dorothy had decided we were made for each other. Naturally, Zena stoutly resisted such a suggestion and I was still semi-attached at the time. But we would be married on 8 May 1948, once I had detached her from a number of wealthy and/or well-connected suitors. I had taken the first steps, late in 1947, on the road to St Simon Zelotes, the little Chelsea church in which we were married.

As I write *1947* it takes me back to New Year's Eve 1946. Zena and I had been out together and I suppose had returned to my flat where I must have received a phone call (no mobiles in those days) telling me that Dick had been in some sort of street accident and was in hospital and in a very serious condition. Later, I discovered that he had left his girlfriend in their flat while he went to find a taxi, when he was struck by a car. They were going to a fancy dress party – he as a schoolboy complete with blazer and cap. It added a bizarre problem to his identification. Thinking back, the call may have come from my mother. We went to the hospital – I think it was The Royal Free where Dick lay. I could see that his life was near its end. I believe the doctors told me that he had an hour or two left. We left the hospital and plunged into crowds, singing, rowdy and rejoicing. The contrast with our own mood seemed particularly cruel, like some rather corny film script. We clung to each other. I think that was our point of no return. I had to go and break the news to my mother. 'It's the curse on the Jews!' she cried. As I've grown old, I've often thought about this. Her much loved brother Bernard had disappeared and one day she showed me some official communication

Zena.

she'd had, stating that he had died 'by gas in Auschwitz'. (But apparently not, according to Holocaust-denier David Irving.)

At the inquest on 'a well-nourished young man of twenty-five', three witnesses, including two bus drivers, claimed that Dick's killer, driving a large Daimler, had gone through a red light at about 45 mph in a 30 mph area, hitting Dick as he crossed where his light was green. Even so, his penalty? Fined £8 and his licence endorsed. He slunk from the court, avoiding our gaze. Bé told me she used to send him a card at Christmas, 'reminding him of his murder'. It snowed on the day of Dick's funeral at Brompton Cemetery where he is buried just by the grave of Richard Tauber.

I had continued to see Clare from time to time. She had never previously regarded our marriage as possible but had now changed her mind. By now, however, I couldn't contemplate life without my unique Canadian. Clare and I had gone through turbulent times together but parting, though painful, did turn out best for us both.

Wedding day, 8 May 1948.

One final digression: in 2002 I saw the long obituary notice of Prebendary Donald Mossman who had married us as the Vicar of St Simon Zelotes (a position he took up in 1942 after heroic work in the Blitz).

I was then on the handsome salary of ten pounds a week. Zena, at this time working for Trans Canada Airlines, made a couple of hundred a year more than me. She had moved from the far west of Canada to Washington, DC, where, in the war, she had worked for the British Air Commission. Her adored younger brother had joined the RCAF and been killed in a crash in 1942. He's buried at Littlehampton, joined many years later by his father's ashes. Zena sailed to England with several Canadian women friends in 1946. She loved England. She wrote vivid letters home for much of her life, and they give a strong sense of her mind and character.

Dick, December 1940.

I like London immensely. It is vast, sprawling, dirty, fascinating – and so old. I work down in the City section of London which is the oldest part. The men who work in the City are a strange collection. All of them wear dark suits, black homburgs or bowlers, gloves and they carry well-rolled black silk umbrellas, rain or shine.

The man I know is a solicitor and while he is most intelligent, well-informed and charming, he has no warmth. What I mean is that he glitters very nicely but the effect is dazzling and chilly rather than comfortable. I have an idea that he finds me a little vulgar but enjoys the novelty.

I hadn't realised that London had been knocked around so badly. In the city especially, the desolation is much worse than I had expected. I work only a few minutes away from St Paul's and for blocks around the cathedral there is just nothing except the foundations of the buildings left. You see eerie sights, like a wall, quite unharmed, and with office notices still pinned up on it, all alone and with grass and even flowers growing through the bricks around it.

Zena's brother, Alec.

English restaurants at the moment, I find, run to atmosphere, poor food, and expensive and scarce liquor. Ordinarily this is not so, or so I have been told, but at present I would just as rather eat at home. I have been dancing only once at a place called Hatchetts on Piccadilly with one of the colonels. The orchestra leader came over to have a drink with us and sat staring fixedly at my legs. I was just beginning to think that perhaps they were better than I had always believed when he said, still staring, 'Tell me, are those *really* nylons?'

We have done an awful lot of sightseeing. Usually on the weekends we get on a bus and ride all over the countryside. I can't attempt to describe the things I have seen but I can tell you where I have been. So far we have visited Oxford, Windsor, Arundel (the seat of the Duke of Norfolk), Littlehampton, Canterbury, Kew Gardens, Westminster Abbey, The Houses of Parliament, the Tower, the Monument, all of the London parks and palaces – I think that is about all. Places like the little towns I have seen are just exactly what Hollywood and postcards show English villages to be. You rather expect that if you were to

Above: Zena's mother Jessie Urquhart with her parents, c. 1898.

Left: Zena, 1917.

Zena's sister Roie, 1982.

return the next day you might find a different set there. The castles really do look like stage sets, especially if you see them with their towers and turrets outlined against the sky. And everything is so very old. I remember dropping into one pub in Canterbury and noticing an unobtrusive little plaque behind one of the doors announcing that it had been established in 1430.

The London parks are quite wonderful. They have beautiful gardens of course but what I really like is to see the flowers growing in the grass. Just around Easter, Hyde Park and Kensington Gardens were carpeted with daffodils, primroses and narcissus. Right now Regents Park is the best because all the tulips given the British Government by the Dutch are in bloom, simply acres of them in every imaginable colour.

When I read this, I realise what splendid letter-writers 'my' women have been. I've already mentioned Clare in the war. Zena and I tried to exchange daily letters when we were apart. And Zena was an assiduous correspondent. The clacking of her typewriter was a familiar sound as she regularly wrote to her beloved sister, Roie, and her family in Vancouver, New Zealand and Rhodesia, and friends all over the world.

Mervyn Francis in Portugal.

Carey (Francis) Ormrod.

As I begin to write about my post-war years, I also realise how lucky I've been in my friends. Sadly, I'm the only survivor of my school friends, but I still spend weekly time with my old Battery Commander, Bill French, whose wife, all unknown to me, was for years a bridge-playing friend of Zena's. The connection only became identified through a chance meeting in the doctor's surgery. Above all, there is the young ex-RAF navigator I met in 1947. Mervyn Francis flew with Coastal Command in Whitleys – notoriously undependable old bombers. He was stationed at St Eval in Cornwall, where the church contains a beautiful stained glass window based on the 39th Psalm: 'the wings of the morning to the uttermost parts of the sea ...'. Mervyn's Whitley inevitably crashed. He survived but has paid with a lifetime's back pain. After the war he worked at BOAC – the forerunner to BA today – but then joined Foote Cone & Belding, the advertising agency in which I worked. The years we have spent together .... our holidays in Cornwall and in Portugal in Mervyn's villa. Numerous evenings when, like the late George Brown, we have been 'tired and emotional'. In short, sixty-four closely interwoven years in which our families survived holidays together, triumph and disaster. I still call his daughter Carey my goddaughter and think of her as such. Indeed it was Carey who was the first person outside the family I told of Zena's fatal illness. I think we both shed tears.

About Foote Cone & Belding: the three gentleman had broken away from their agency (featured in an American book called *The Hucksters* by Frederick Wakeman) to form their own. We novices in London knew little of their serpentine activities. Fairfax ('Fax') Cone seemed to be the mainspring. Eleven years later, in October 1958, I was to send him a memo of farewell:

As your Oldest Inhabitant (London), I should not wish to leave FCB without sending you a personal farewell.

I recall that my duties over these twelve years and more, have included operating a three-line switchboard (very difficult) and gazing enchanted upon Fujyama (very easy). In a way these recollections typify the wide range of interests FCB has had to offer since we operated in one apartment; and, believe me, I do not leave without sentimental stirrings of the heart.

Unfortunately, the path of my own ambition and interests does not appear to coincide with that which I can expect to tread in FCB; so today I have to write and say goodbye. I have tried to give the Company the best I had in me – and certainly I recognise that it has given me much in return; all of which has, I hope, made for an amicable parting. And I shall certainly miss your Blue Streaks!

My very sincere personal regards.

To which he replied, rather more tersely:

Dear Jack

   It was nice of you to write me.

   I am sorry you are leaving Foote, Cone & Belding.

   But I wish you everything good.

   Fax

Pat Dolan's secretary told me that when Emerson Foote came to London, he cried and told her he just wanted to write some copy. This bizarre kind of behaviour was not all that unusual in those days. Don Belding pursued some shadowy pursuits on the West Coast of USA.

Our office was in Davis Street almost next door to Claridge's. We often saw King Hussein of Jordan who was rumoured to have a mistress there. Another noteworthy sighting was the beautiful actress Deborah Kerr who was just achieving fame. Later we moved to Charles Street, where my military skills were employed getting the office furnished. I remember it was 1947. We were all dreadfully cold 'from morn till dewy eve' – except Pat Dolan who cheerfully commandeered a large electric fire on which he kept all three bars going all day. Few things have given me more satisfaction than the letter I got three months after I joined FCB, from John Cuff the General Manager: all were very pleased with my progress in establishing an overseas dept. My pay was raised to £750 pa (I heard a news item today about a modest footballer in a modest team, who was paid *only* £15,000 a week.) What mad, heady days marked my early advertising life! We had the RKO account and handled their blockbuster film *Duel in the Sun* – or 'Dool' as an American executive used to call it. *We* called it Lust in the Dust. (With some difficulty we dissuaded a slightly mad American from stampeding a herd of cattle down Piccadilly.) We had an American account executive who was married to a rather glamorous West End singing star. It was rumoured that he would have – possibly even already had – poisoned his mother to advance his career. Then there was Glenda, the girl who, it was said, took the L out of public relations and the print manager whose life was devoted to collecting Christmas presents from our suppliers. When Pat took me on, we numbered less than a dozen, but by the time he left to set up his own Agency somewhere around 1950, there must have been fifty or sixty at least. He had fallen out with his American colleagues, who frequently sent over their head of international affairs, Harry Berk. His main goal appeared to be the undermining and destruction of Pat. I still acted as an occasional confidential chauffeur, at which point deadly secrets might be imparted by them both. Pat took a few key staff with him, but didn't ask me to go, and may have been inhibited from doing so by loyalty to colleagues; something we still believed in back then. He was succeeded by Brian McCabe who had been Mervyn's boss at BOAC. A former tank commander awarded an MC with the Eighth Army in the Desert, Brian was an energetic charismatic character. We got on very well at first, but – and I never quite figured out why – I gradually fell out of favour. I think he didn't consider me serious enough about my work – successful though it proved to be. Also, he felt very strongly that when we visited clients we should wear a *hat* – something I unwisely resisted for too long; though eventually a trip to Herbert Johnson (my quondam army cap supplier) in Bond Street produced a brown thing which didn't suit me at all, and usually I carried it. Black mark.

If our relationship soured somewhat, it was still important to me. Hence a second, personalised letter when I left FCB in 1958:

Dear Brian

I feel I don't wish to leave FCB without sending you a short note, and what I want to say is this: That although we may not have seen everything the same way over the years, I have always been well aware that it was to you that I owed my big chance in the company. In the event, I may not have turned out to be quite the person you expected. Be that as it may, I believe you'll agree that I have put my best into FCB, and I shall leave behind me something of value.

All of which should add up to my leaving in a friendly atmosphere; and I should indeed be sorry if that weren't so.

To which he replied:

Dear Jack

Very many thanks for your memo of 5.11.58.

I would certainly hate you to leave with any sort of misunderstanding about my feelings. There is no doubt whatever in my mind that you have done an absolutely first-class job. You have worked conscientiously, efficiently and hard – and have made a great contribution to the company's success.

As to what you 'might have been', please put down any criticisms I have made as being inevitable by 'the very nature of the beast' – the 'beast' being me. I am afraid I was born with an irrepressible urge to improve things. Consequently I am rarely satisfied all the time with anything or anyone – very much including myself! It must be very wearing on people who don't grow to understand my nature, and it is certainly wearing on me, but it does not mean, because I'm periodically urging people to do better, that I don't appreciate what they have done. And I do appreciate what you have done.

I don't suppose I have really explained it, but anyway, the very best of luck with CPV, and thank you for all you have done.

Brian

Brian was an outstanding person, but was a poor judge of people. I urged him to make my number two my successor but he chose someone with a meretricious CV who clearly wasn't the right person. He was discarded fairly soon; and my number two duly appointed – and successful!

Brian had made me Manager of the Overseas Department in FCB London and so it came about that in 1948 I was sent on the first of my many overseas tasks; this time to Cairo on the BOAC business which Brian had brought to the Agency. It was exciting. The only proper plane I'd ever been in was the DC3 which had flown me, malaria-stricken, out of the Normandy bridgehead some four years before. Here I was in a four-engined York (a civilian version of the Lancaster) as, saluted by the lined-up ground staff (can you believe this?) we taxied out to the runway at Heathrow, then a few nissen huts and tents. We stopped at well-remembered Tripoli where, on the rain-swept tarmac, I met a school contemporary whom I hardly knew – and never saw again. Ah, to be back in Cairo with its distinctive spice-and-petrol smell in the heat. I had drinks, and the inevitable peanuts, at Shepheards but I didn't stay there. In fact, although I made a number of visits, I never stayed at Shepheards again as it was destroyed by fire in 1952. But I was touched by memories of 1942, and the words of that famous song: 'Oh, how the memory clings, these foolish things ...'.

Then another one of my life's Jewish episodes. In those days if you wanted to visit Israel on business (which, indeed, I did) you had to have a separate passport as the Arabs denied you entry if your passport contained an Israeli stamp. Also, you had to travel via Cyprus. Everyone knew what was going on, but the charade was maintained. As it happened, I had invited to dinner some weeks before the brother-in-law of a friend at work. This person, who was called Leslie Toogood, after a good dinner settled down to demolish a bottle of whisky. Growing expansively cordial, he explained that he was in the Arab Legion (a small but reportedly formidable force raised in Jordan, commanded by Major General John Glubb – 'Glubb Pasha' – and staffed by British Officers, largely faux-Lawrences and ex-Palestine police.

Jack's mother with
Richard, 1958.

The Arab Legion had singularly failed to see off the Israelis in their war of
independence.) This Mr Toogood (indeed ex-Palestine police) or Lieutenant-
Colonel Toogood as we were informed, had some sort of pay corps
function. He preferred to express it as, 'you could call me the Chancellor
of the Exchequer of the Arab Legion.' Anyway, when very late and suitably
lubricated, he finally left. He insisted that if ever I were in Jordan I should
visit him in the mess and one day I was to do so. But first: Israel. Our Dakota
lumbered from Nicosia to Lod, the plane stopped, and after it had been
sprayed with some disinfectant, in stepped a ravishing Israeli girl. Eyes and
teeth flashing, 'Welcome to Israel' she hailed us. The state was only a few
weeks old and I found it an emotional moment. And like Portnoy I found it
rather extraordinary that all the people were Jews instead of their usual role
of – by and large – a respectful minority.

I managed to get my work done in spite of residual ill feelings after the
British mandate, the bombing of the King David Hotel etc, and still found
time to visit Jerusalem and the Wailing Wall as well as the biblical Seven
Stations of the Cross, the Mount of Olives, Bethlehem and the Church of
the Nativity and the Dead Sea. I also got down to Beersheba and the Negev
Desert as well as collecting a nasty sunburn. Then to Amman, the capital
of Jordan and in those days quite a modest, suburban sort of place. Here I
did indeed visit the officers' mess of the Arab Legion and had to listen when

With Richard Laing
Swaab, 1956.

a number of these warriors denigrated the doings of 'The Yids' across the border. I suppose I should have pointed out that a Yid of sorts was enjoying their hospitality but I maintained a cowardly silence. ('Sufferance is the badge of all our tribe!') I don't recount this encounter with pride, though I recognise that any sort of minor heroics would have been pointless. The people across the border had already had the last word. But this was the last occasion on which, for me, discretion was to be the better part of valour.

I came home, bringing Zena some star sapphire earrings from the Souk, to some very bad news. Zena had suffered the first of her miscarriages, at three months. She – we – were to undergo this heartbreak three more times in the coming years, until in 1955 along came our first born – a son, Richard Laing, names which mingled elements of both our families. Our whole road rejoiced. I hung a yellow ribbon on the tree in our garden. Only our Siamese cat was not best pleased. I had to put a net on the pram as it stood in the courtyard, to avoid a feline desire to share the warm space. The nuns at St Theresa's where Richard was born, regarded him after the earlier disasters, as a small miracle. So did we. But as I returned home to our first crushing disappointment all this lay ahead of us. And a year or so later, in February 1952, fate had another little surprise in store: TB. I'd just returned again from the Middle East including Syria where, in Damascus, I managed to find the narrow street with the entrance thought to be 'the eye of a needle' so difficult for a camel to negotiate according to Mark and Matthew's Gospels. Nasty cough. Blood. And an X-ray confirming TB on the right apex of my lung. I had to stop work immediately and Zena moved one of the beds next to the window where I lay for the next sixteen weeks awaiting a sanatorium vacancy. I drank two pints of warm milk a day and swallowed ten enormous cachets of INAH, a new treatment. I was also exceedingly lucky to be one of the first recipients of the new, life-saving wonder drug, Streptomycin. The district nurses whacked an injection into one side or other of my skinny buttocks at regular intervals; and after two months I had put an amazing eight pounds on to my increasingly scraggy body. As I lay in bed, life in the street became a passing show, a theatre. We always enjoyed 'laughing Goalen', a lovely neighbour who closely resembled Barbara the famous model. I think I was the object of some curiosity as TB in those days was still dangerous, if not the death sentence of so much fiction. Then came word of a place in a sanatorium .... in Ventnor, Isle of Wight, where at some point in the war I had been posted for invasion duty and slept (fitfully) in a beach hut, Tommy gun (supposedly) ready to repel some brawny Nazi commando. (Why should England tremble? We used to joke, grimly.)

CHAPTER 8

1952. TB AND THE SANATORIUM

Though set among palm trees on the cliffs above the sea, the line of blocks of the Royal National Hospital presented a forbidding Dickensian, institutional appearance which presumably led me on 23 May 1952 to start the first of the seventy-one letters I sent to Zena:

> Dearest Zene let me out of here! I must admit I am having to struggle hard against severe depression, but I don't doubt that is a normal enough reaction... I am resolutely ignoring what all the other patients tell me about how long they have been in as they all indicated that 6 months is the likely minimum. However, until I've been to see the doctor I shan't speculate.

I went on to explain that I was on 'Bed' which entailed getting up only for washing or going to the loo, and that the next stage was 'up 2 hours'. I add a few details – and reactions:

> 12.30. I have been doing my morning 'rest' hour during which no speaking or writing is allowed. There are 2 others in the afternoon – as you see, it's an exciting life. I've been watching the buses run past and thinking how little healthy people realise how lucky they are. I didn't give it a thought myself. This morning too I was X-rayed again but I haven't seen Dr Miller yet.

Letter 2 is inexplicably missing, but in no. 3, by which time I've found out more rules about visiting times, use of radio (on *battery* only and *quietly*; hospital radio closes at 9.30). I sympathise on her 'good howl' on returning home and say I felt like it myself. I explain that after 'up 2 hours', comes 'up 6 hours'. I give her details of further treatment:

The Royal National Hospital in Ventnor.

This morning I had the gastric lavage which is a kind of stomach pump. The trick is to try and relax while swallowing about 3 feet of rubber tubing which makes you retch, heave and cry and cough and the whole thing is most undignified and uncomfortable. I had the hell of a job and after getting it half way once coughed it all up again. When down they syringe up the most revolting phlegm and stuff which has to be tested for positive or negative. I think I'll be better at it next time. I don't think you would be awfully good at it – so be careful!.

Then, my second encounter with the Head Physician, Dr Alexander Miller. (He had examined me, and I was quite amazed by the touch of his hands as he probed my back and chest):

Dr Miller was doing rounds this morning (as our ward doctor is on holiday) and we discussed GL. He said to sister 'I once passed some tubing down an unconscious chap and would you believe it he coughed it up tied in a knot.' I said 'He must have been a Boy Scout' (rather smily) and M thought it was quite funny. M either had or has TB himself. He's very nice though very strict.

In letter 4 I explain the Damoclean situation of positive or negative sputum tests. Life was really governed by this until the day you left:

I want to try and explain more about the complaint to you, which may make things clearer. The whole key to the thing is whether your sputum is negative or positive. They dredge it up from your stomach to get enough and get it early. Now it can either show positive immediately or they grow a culture from it and it is negative if nothing has turned up in 6 weeks. The degree of activity is roughly determined by the length of time it takes to get a positive (or stay negative). They do their best to get a positive by growing the culture in the ideal conditions for the bug so if you get through without a positive you can be bloody sure TB isn't active.

I mention this to show you how we have got to acquire a frame of mind which must be prepared for a positive at any time. It won't mean I won't get better – don't think that. It may mean a small operation and it will mean longer in here. On the other hand if I am healing well and not at all active I may never get a positive. I shall have gastric lavage every three weeks or so I expect. Don't be too alarmed about talk of a cavity. All the infiltrations are cavities after all. It doesn't mean they have to go very deep and it doesn't mean they aren't healed or healing. Also I may be wrong about staying in bed that long. It will depend on the results of the tomogram. I'm afraid my earlier letters have betrayed too much of the depression I felt on coming here. Things are gradually better. More people come to see me, I get letters and papers and books and – a source of great joy – the birds feed from my sill – chaffinches and one special blackbird comes right in the room. He was in here early this morning chirping away and taking the bread I leave for him.

I spent hours watching the birds a mere foot or two away on my window sill. By letter 5, I am writing:

I assure you I have been far more cheerful and I felt my letters were one long moan. Now I am getting adjusted and although the evenings are rather depressing and filled with what I call 'Mimi thoughts' (*La Bohème* ...) I am no longer quite so appalled by the possibilities of a longer stay. The human being is astonishingly resilient. Nevertheless I am still hoping to do it in 4 months or so. The birds are a great joy. Yesterday I had the blackbird and his mate in here on the window seat. The female sang and sang and I was absolutely enthralled. She is rather shy though and although I put more bread out she wouldn't come back. Mr. was here at 6 o'clock though, tapping away at the bread. Mind you get something to eat before you get here on Saturday. You'll feel lousy if you starve yourself. It certainly will be good to see you – I think you're probably right to have decided to come down as my morale will be boosted.

Wu Ling.

I now get Mr & Mrs and Miss (or Master) blackbird in here and today Mr actually fed the young one beak to beak. I hardly dared breathe.

In these early days I miss home and Wu Ling our Siamese cat. However, Zena has started to visit, and I write on Whit Monday:

I sometimes try and improve morale by visualising the moment of my return to the cottage. Undoubtedly my mental picture will be belied by events for it always appears to be high summer (God forbid!) and somewhere lurking discreetly but definitely behind windows, fences and hedges are the imbecile grins of nearly all our friends! Wu Ling leaps to my shoulder from the middle of the lawn and the MGM choir is singing *One Fine Day* (or possibly *Some Enchanted Evening*) from the Newmans' flat.

I do hope Wu Ling was OK on your return. It's awful that he, I or all of us have to be browned off to keep the others happy. Still he should be comfortable and he's well fed so he'll just have to think of poor Bimmie and think himself lucky he's not in a sanatorium with only fish pieces and uncreamy milk for a diet with a very occasional scrap of rabbit.

Much love to you and greetings to anybody I like.

Your loving Bim.

We were rather hard up as my office pay had been cut by 50% (to the disgust of my friends at *Time Life* who wanted to make up the difference.) Luckily my rich Uncle George in Genoa helped out. Zena considered taking in a paying guest but fortunately it didn't come to that. On the 12 June came a landmark:

Later: Grading is over. Miller said 'I see they're still fattening you up in spite of the good food you had at home', and then after a pause 'Well you're within a week of getting up' which gives me something definite to look forward to.

Life wasn't easy for Zena. The journey to the IOW was tiring, the visits short and uncertainty hung over us. On Friday 13 June I wrote:

Don't get depressed; as you say it won't last for ever and other people have worse luck after all. (You have only to talk to some of them in here to realise that.) Keep your pecker up therefore!

Much love to you and Wu Ling the bold slayer of aggressive birds.

On 16 June there was rather an interesting little footnote to Pat Dolan and his exit from FCB:

Frankly dear I would not advise seeing Pat. I think it is rather absurd to advise against it but bearing in mind the way Brian is and the attitude he has taken towards us, I wouldn't like to risk offending him – specially knowing the way these things get misrepresented by gossip. Remember Pat himself told Bill B that I had decided to work for him (Pat) when I'd done nothing of the kind. As to the new drugs, it is kind of Pat but (a) I shall be given them here if it is necessary and (b) we could get them easily enough via Elly, FCB, Walter and a number of other sources.

I was going through a fretful stage:

I'm going through rather a bored and impatient phase at present. It's so unnatural to lie in bed all day when you feel well and strong and in midsummer. Don't tell me all the answers because of course I know them already, but sometimes even though you know what is necessary it isn't always easy to do it. For example often in the war you could see a bit of ground erupting under enemy shell fire and you knew you had to pass through it to reach the objective. Well you did – but you didn't necessarily enjoy it even though you knew you had to do it.

Warmest love to Wu Ling and you from your loving (and sensitive and brilliant)
Bimmie.

The fine man wot eleven stonekins weighs!

Bim was Zena's pet name for me and I begin to use some of our special language which I developed over the years. We called it Swaabese.

I was making good progress. On 19 June I reported:

Miller said to Sless, 'Ah yes we're having him X-rayed again'. 'Yes', said Sless 'And then we hope to get him up,' said M, so I hope to be up soon – especially as I had rather expected to be today. Miller seemed pleased (and surprised) that I was continuing to gain weight. He didn't expect me to, having already gained so much at home. Or that's more or less what he said. He checked with sister that they have nothing positive out of me – and they haven't. Yet ...

Some days I worried whether all the travelling was too much for Zena:

Evening rest hour is over and I thought I'd start my tomorrow's letter; by now I imagine you are on the London bound train – and not I do hope, too uncomfortable. Undoubtedly you have the worst of it when the visits are over with a long journey back, and I certainly wish I could do something to help, but of course that's impossible for the time being.

2 hours certainly can pass fast can't they? Still it was certainly worth it to me – though I didn't have to make that big journey twice. I really think that unless you can get Al and Nancy to oblige you'd better skip next Sunday.

On 3 July came a big day:

Miller has just been in. No comments but I have got 2 and 1. Do you realise this means I shall now dress, walk all the way to the dining hall, and eat my tea in mixed (but I gather strictly separated!) company. Life as she is lived, eh?

When I wrote no. 2 on 5 July, I had to explain that I was on Paul Bunyan's bed while he borrowed my room. His wife was visiting and (as I did for Dr Geoff James, a fellow patient, and his mistress(es)) I lent my room for sex. (It was one of the relatively few singles. In due course Zena and I needed it for ourselves.) I also described my first day on 2 and 1:

Well, yesterday I was dressed (couldn't do up the fastening by at least 2 inches on my older Daks) and went to the dining hall for the first time. It felt pretty queer after so long in comparative solitude. Strict segregation and the atmosphere was heavy with bread and butter and lustful glances! There were

At Ventnor Sanatorium, 1953. Smithy, Jack, Paul, Frank.

in fact a few quite attractive girls among the 2 or 3 dozen in hall and of course at this stage almost anything looks attractive!

The summer days passed, marked by the so-important variations in bodily temperature, weight gain, the Damocelan GL sputum specimens and progress: 2 hours up then 7 and 3, 9 and 3, and that first important target: ADR (All Day Rest which wasn't exactly rest, but didn't include 'walks' which came later). I made some good friends: Frank Evans, wonderfully camp and amusing and (though, stupidly, I didn't realise it) gay. Geoff James the doctor I've mentioned, who finally got my room W21 for his vigorous sexual activity. Paul Bunyan, one of our bridge four; Donald Corbet-Smith and his sweet young wife, Brenda; Smithie who had a setback in sight of the finishing post. I moved to E Block, a stepping stone towards the Exit. I shared a room with Frank which was a real joy. After meeting Zena he said, 'what a pleasure to talk to a sophisticated woman,' and Geoff (he'd had polio) called her, 'charming and attractive'. I passed all these compliments on to her. On 27 July:

Stan Fawns (the hairless) has just been in making complimentary remarks about you. I am to tell you he 'has fallen in love with your accent'! I'm afraid you'll be getting too conceited if you come down here much more often!

E Block was pleasant. I wrote:

I am really liking life in E Block. It is very different from W. Hardly any supervision and you no longer have a hospital atmosphere. It's more like a sort of very restful holiday camp without the Billy Butlin effects! If it weren't for the fact that I'm anxious to get home it would be almost enjoyable.

Or as Frank put it as we lounged in our deckchairs in the sunshine: 'Thank god for TB'. By 13 August I mention a couple more milestones:

... a lovely soft morning and I went duly down to breakfast for the first time. Felt pretty good but there's a lot of day to be got through when it starts that early.

I think I shall probably go on the coach trip on Saturday – it is to Sandown via Shanklin. It'll feel pretty strange among all the holidaymakers.

I was indeed able to get out and in my letter 45 I described my day:

Saturday 8.30 pm: Well it was very nice getting out. Geoff and I pottered round the shops buying things and ogling the shop girls, bought prawns and sat on a breakwater to eat them and had a cuppa and cake and ice cream. I bought some odds and ends (I forgot the Dr Page Barker hair tonic) such as a teapot for Frank and me, a new toothbrush, a duster and some Kiwi – and some Bigren oil which I'll give you on Tuesday! We had half an hour in Shanklin (it rained most of it) and an hour in Sandown. I tried to get you some net nylons but both places were almost out of all nylons. I cast a reminiscent eye over the Regina and the Sally Lunn but the chap with 'hit the little devils on the head; they must go in' was not functioning. It amused me to see that one thing at least doesn't change: the behaviour of small boys on the sands. Anyway it all made a very pleasant change and we all got back very cheerful and contented. (97.6 and 68 by the way). I had a very large supper – basically rabbit and potatoes, plus (privately) lettuce and tomato and cheese and brown bread and butter. Geoff managed to wheedle some butter from a grocer in Sandown; very skilful. Frank is just doing his exercises and I have had a delicious bath so we are both all set for boody lippis we hope. I expect to see Brenda briefly tomorrow and I expect I can get news of you from her.

My first encounter with this gentleman was on a boyhood holiday described in chapter 1. Amazing that after so many years, the ping pong ball man was still there though ('not functioning') on the day. Apart, of course, from my separation, life was now becoming quite pleasant:

I expect [Frank] he'll move in today or tomorrow to 15. This is a delightful room: sunny and quite warm and you can see the sea from your pillow. Also very easy to sweep out and keep clean. I really like it in here and, as far as circumstances permit, feel very contented.

I am now going walkies and will finish this off later. Walkies! imagine ..... Later: Had a very pleasant walk. It is a simply glorious morning – warm and soft, and the grounds are quite delightful – woods and mossy paths etc. I have more walks of course this afternoon.

We had (Frank, Geoff, Smithie and I) a most pleasant balcony supper (Hall was Hideous Haddock) of *hors d'oeuvre* (sardine, tomato, cucumber, dressing), franks and brown bread and butter, a super fruit (canned and fresh) salad with sherry in it and cheese and biscuits and chocolates. Such a spread of course merited my weekly cigarette. Then I had a bath, warmed my milk and am about to drink it feeling that it has been a most excellent day and the kind on which nobody in his right mind actively grumbles about being in a sanatorium.

I hope you'll continue to get better quickly and that Wu will be reasonable about learning to use his Wu door.

Much love to you both from your Bim

Wot iss hemissy though (small) teebeekins hass.

On the 1 September came a real milestone:

No particular comment from Miller; just asked if I was managing all right. If nothing goes wrong (ie culture) we can almost reckon on my being home in about a month. Usually you do 3 weeks on 15s – often 2 on 15 'in' and 1 on 15 'out' and then a final week on 30s. So without counting any unhatched chickens a certain optimism is I think permissible.

Thereafter, every letter dwelt on the wonderful prospect of returning home, linked with the need not to count chickens before hatching. Here is a long one from very near the end of my sanatorium time.

I shall be calling on some more physical stamina tomorrow, when I start my 15s, though as a matter of fact I don't expect them to be very much more effort than the 10s – specially as I've done an occasional 15 already. I look forward to your letter in the morning because it'll be the one giving your reaction to my getting 15s – which I imagine must have come as a pleasant surprise to you. My 3rd culture is 6 weeks old tomorrow or the next day so barring any very unusual bad luck we should soon only have the 4th one to worry about!

Well dear, Rest Hour looms so I must end. I try not to contemplate too often the possibility that we may not have to write letters for much longer.

Much love to you and Wu from your Bim.

Wot Funfteens ootaymommis make will.

I am glad Jack Laidlaw was so optimistic though after some time in here I am still inclined to be cautious about cultures having seen some pretty odd things happening. But I do believe that barring some freak of ill fortune I shall now be all right. It will be wonderful to be home again and to be able to forget about TB (within reason). I am sick of being an invalid though I've no grumbles about being here if I've got to be anywhere.

I'd certainly like to see Monica but I suggest it'd be a good idea if she were to come with you on what we hope will be your last visit, ie the one after the weekend of the 20th.

These days I find it difficult to think of much beyond the fact that I may actually be home in 3 or 4 (preferably 3) weeks. What with that and the car and everything, life is going to be very good I feel.

This afternoon out on the cliff the sky seemed full of swallows flying round and round apparently aimlessly. I imagine they were making a rendezvous for their southward flights to warmer shores; it served as a reminder that the year is growing older. It's hard to remember the spring as I watched it from my bed though I definitely can recall the top of our lime tree growing greener and greener each day, and the 'Recitatif' bird – whatever it may have been. Well I hope it won't be too long before I see the lime tree again – and on that note I'll end for today.

Frank hadn't done his walks this afternoon so after evening rest hour I walked him up to the first cliff seat. It was a delightfully mellow evening, the sun still warm enough to be comfortable and the breeze which blows all day fallen with the approach of evening. The sea was calm and blue and we sat purring on the seat for 5 minutes before going back. Really these leisurely days are heaven-sent and were it not for the fear of lurking disaster (ie a positive) would fill one with great content – perhaps I should say greater content for we are fairly happy.

I feel quite fantastically well tonight which in view of the way I live is as should be but is none the less satisfactory. I have a BSR on Monday and another X-ray and routine next week – I hope it will be my last.

I was talking to Auntie this morning and she said she expects (failing any disaster and assuming a good routine) that I shall not have to do 2 weeks on 15 'out' but should get my ticket next Monday, ie tomorrow week. It's a wonderful thought; I suppose one shouldn't start banking on it – but it's difficult not to do so.

Rather good to think that if all goes well this coming weekend may be my last but one. Mind you we mustn't bank on my ticket next Monday but I do think we can classify it as highly probable – always assuming further masterly inactivity by my 4th culture. When I get out of here I don't think I shall ever want to hear the word culture again – in fact I shall reach for my pistol if I do.

Do you realise I shall only be writing today and tomorrow as there's no point in doing so on Friday? Rather boody really.

But I must say that with increasing fitness I begin to find the time passing rather slowly – even though rather less than 5 months is a short enough stay really. It is 33 weeks now since I took to bed.

After our phone call little remains to be said except for the ultra boodiness of the thought that I shall (DV) be coming home on 1 October. I have been fantastically lucky compared with so many of the chaps here but 4 1/2 months can be a long time all the same even in the middle of a pleasant summer. I'm not so sure I shall ever want to come to Ventnor again.... [I did return in September 2010 only to find the Sanatorium had been sold, demolished and transformed into tropical gardens – plus caff.]

I hardly believe it's true but it's only 8 complete days away. Boody boody. On that note I'll end but I'll add some more in the morning specially as I shall by then have your letter on which to comment. Boody nymis.

I saw Sless last night and he told me that the X-ray they took on Monday is virtually clear and healed. He said you have to scrutinise it extremely closely to see anything at all in the way of a shadow. I certainly seem to have healed well.

I also realise that except for next Monday this should be my last letter from the San – as you're coming down on Sunday I shan't be writing on Saturday or Sunday itself.

Rest hour is about to take place so I'll end. What a fantastically boody thought that this should be the last letter but one that I write you from here.

Sunday, 28 Sept. 8.40pm. Dearest Zene. I begin what I hope will be my last letter to you from here. I can hardly believe I've only two more days in here. A most unreasoning terror of my 4th culture (in spite of all the evidence) hangs over me and I shall be glad to leave. I could have borne the last 2 weeks with far greater equanimity had it not been for that damn thing in the laboratory. Mind you all the other people on ticket also have cultures on – and all have the same feeling about them; so do 9/10 of the other people in E Block. You have a horrible feeling that whatever your personal condition the law of averages catch up on you! However, away with such ideas – am sure all will be well – or if not sure, hopeful.

...and that only leaves tomorrow, which with Ventnor, packing, final farewells and the excitement of 'home tomorrow' should be quite bearable.

And on that forward looking note, I think I'll end my (once again, I HOPE) final sanatorium letter. The day after tomorrow I hope to see you and Wu Ling again – and this time without any time limit!

Much love to you both from your Bim.

Wot homekin makes!

So, in that autumn of 1952, I returned home. I did feel a great thankfulness at being able to live a 'normal' daily life, with all its problems and pleasures. And many of each lay ahead. And now, as I approach that fateful Ides of March for the 93rd time, I am (as you'd expect) often preoccupied with thoughts of death. My attitude has changed since I wrote in my diary on 19 October 1944:

> Last night in bed I was thinking about life and death and it suddenly occurred to me that though people talk a lot about it, when you actually think to yourself: 'in this next attack I may actually die – and find out about Heaven and Hell, and completely and suddenly end as far as this life's concerned' – Well it's a different matter . It's as well one doesn't think that way too often because it's rather frightening in a deep, disturbing way. So it's better just to look on the forthcoming battle as just another battle and not go too far into details.

In 2005 after an operation, a severe infection put me in danger; one of the doctors told Richard that the following few hours could prove decisive. I remember feeling a sort of unworried resignation, certainly not fear. Recently I read an article by someone who had recovered from a severe cancer. He said – and I share his feelings – that he didn't so much fear death as the process of dying. However, he added, he would probably be leaving in a haze of diamorphine – maybe the best way to go. I could never identify with Sassoon's outburst:

> Oh Jesus give me a wound today
> And I'll believe in your bread and wine
> And get my bloody old sins washed white

although if I'd been in the trenches in the First World War I might have. There was a saying in my war, attributed I think to an American *padre*: 'There are no atheists in foxholes,' which I always thought rather feeble and self-serving.

CHAPTER 9

1953-68. RAISING A FAMILY, MAKING A NAME, SEEING THE WORLD

When I returned at last to London nearly sixty years ago, we had a beautiful young queen and Winston was Prime Minister but times were still hard. For the first few months I worked part-time, but life was made very much easier thanks to the car (an Austin A40) which my mother had given me. (In Swaabese this car was always called 'the Ah Ho'.) When I got ill, my friend Mervyn (who, I note, was our second overnight visitor at our recently purchased cottage on 31 August 1949) and I made a pact: we would see the Ashes Test at Lord's in 1953. And, sitting in the Mound stand, we did; though my memory seems only to recall our batsman helpless in the face of the hurricane that fell upon them from Lindwall and Keith Miller. Of course, in those days cricketers played in caps, not helmets, or, like Denis Compton, bare-headed. In due course both Mervyn and I became MCC members and were able to watch from the hallowed pavilion; though I never reached the exalted privilege of my own reserved seat which he did – right by the gate. That year, my parents-in-law from Vancouver spent four summer months with us. As a great treat we hired a small black and white TV so that they were able to watch the Coronation. Zena's Canadian connections here in London enabled her to get them an invitation to a Buckingham Palace garden party, and I still have a photograph of them with a London bobby. After Zena's father died, her mother lived with us from December 1968 to December the following year. She and our boys doted on one another and it was a happy consolation for her loss of Hector.

Because everything was so new and different after the war years, the next decade was one of the most interesting of my life. I travelled widely, usually flying first class on BOAC which was my client. Once, on a two-deck Boeing Stratocruiser, in company with a BOAC executive who'd been a war-time wing commander, our travelling companion was Douglas Bader who was working for one of the big international companies – I think it was Shell. He was extremely entertaining – and very politically incorrect – and, of course, a legend and a very exciting person to meet. I spent time with them both in Bermuda. I was on my way round South America. The journey started inauspiciously with a car journey from the airport to Caracas on a road which had 365 bends. I just avoided throwing up. (This was before they built a road by tunnelling through the mountains. I believe the journey only takes fifteen minutes as against what was it an hour on the old road?) Caracas in those days was thriving; new roads and apartment buildings and something new to me: a supermarket. People used to say, 'meet you at four, after the rain', a punctual daily occurrence. I believe it was when I was leaving at the airport restaurant that I enjoyed a brief exchange with Yma Sumac. This flamboyant and remarkable singer had an international reputation triggered by her extraordinary voice which spanned an amazing four octaves. She was known as The Nightingale of the Andes, having been born in Peru in 1922. Her PR people claimed she was descended from the Inca Kings. There was a scurrilous rumour that she was really Amy Camus from The Bronx. I noticed how dirty within her expensive sandals her toenails were. Yma Sumac died in 2008 in New York.

When I left Caracas I was on a Venezuelan airline – LAV. Remembering some of Bader's comments about their pilots I was rather apprehensive. My feelings were not eased by the knowledge that the Venezuelan War Minister was to be a travelling companion. One side effect of this was the selection of several impossibly glamorous girls as cabin staff – not that they could spare much time for the rest of us. However, we arrived safely in Lima, where, when we disembarked, we saw what must have been a large proportion of the Peruvian armed forces drawn up on the tarmac. I seem to remember martial music and a gun salute. 'Too kind, but you shouldn't have bothered', I remarked facetiously to one of the airline officials. He was not amused, and I was hustled away to the terminal. I only visited Lima once (though Peter walked the Inca Trail to Machu Picchu years later. Terribly dangerous – specially to an asthmatic) and I remember two things, neither of which does me any credit. The first – excusable perhaps – was eating watermelon at dinner. This left me jack-knifing on the bathroom floor the following 2 a.m. The second – certainly not excusable – involved an evening spent drinking a number of *pisco sours*, a tasty but lethal local delicacy. During this evening I seem to have been joined by a most attractive girl. 'You're the image of Princess Margaret', I insisted; more and more frequently as the *pisco sour* worked its evil results. I regret to tell you that (with no memory of the interim) I woke up in 'Princess Margaret's' bed next morning, relieved to be assured that 'nothing had happened' and about to miss my flight.

I was still in the early days of my travel, and I had not yet mastered the art of by-passing inadvisable menus. Thus, when my kind Chilean host one evening urged me to try the small but tasty local oysters, I overlooked several ill-advised brief encounters I'd already had with these subtle but irresistible creatures. 'You must have four dozen,' insisted my kind host, 'because they are so small'. Big mistake. Back in the UK, I only tried oysters once again at impeccable Wheelers. It was the last and spectacularly messy hurrah.

Another unhappy experience was in Hong Kong. I think it was my first visit, and it soon became clear that a large, rich meal was not going to stay with me. I vividly recall how I heaved unhappily into the lavatory and, the vision which I could not banish, of huge glistening pork sausages sizzling in some ghostly frying pan. In those days, Chile still had an Anglo-Latin feel engendered no doubt by memories of Admiral Lord Cochrane, and the Santiago capital was a lovely city. The countryside felt like a sort of glorified England, and I was sorry when the time came to board the DC4 which limped across the snow-covered Andes to Rio with what seemed (peering blearily from the window) about twelve feet to spare. With wider experience, I became rather choosey about which aircraft I enjoyed. Hence I flew with most of the major airlines of the time, some of which no longer exist ... PanAm, TWA (where I had a personalised seat and a Polaroid photo taken on a Royal Ambassador Trans Atlantic flight). Then there were Garuda, SAS, Philippine, Cathay Pacific, Air India, PIA, Japan Airlines, among others.

One flight I *do* remember all too well. I think it was from Rangoon and it was a DC3. For some reason I had in mind the death of the famous American soprano, Grace Moore whose KLM DC3 flight from Copenhagen to Stockholm had ended when the plane, soon after take-off, plunged from 150 feet into the ground. My recollection was that the ground crew had failed to remove the wooden chocks of the ailerons on the wings. When I had looked out of the window I was sure that I hadn't seen our ground crew removing these things. I debated with myself: to say something and probably look stupid? To say nothing and probably end up dead? I called the stewardess and asked her to pass my misgivings to the captain. Giving me an apprehensive glance, she agreed to do so. The dear old Dakota eventually lumbered into the air – and stayed there; though I do recall that over the Burmese mountains we encountered a tremendous thunderstorm. We lurched and tumbled about and I watched the lightning dancing along our wings and I wondered whether I'd been counting premature chickens. The DC3 was, of course, the world's workhorse and had served worldwide in many guises. I once flew in one in the Horn of Africa, in company with a large number of locals – and their livestock. It was not a peaceful journey, starting with the rather odd experience in Eritrea of taking off and *descending*. We had launched off the end of a mountain runway rather like an aircraft carrier. In those days, aeroplanes still had propellers and it wasn't until the first De Havilland Comets had crashed in the mid fifties, that I had my first experience of jet flight. I was in Beirut on BOAC business when the local manager told me that a Comet 2E (the new one) was going on a testing flight to London the next day, and would I like to go. *Would I*? Next morning I left the Hotel St. George where I always stayed and climbed into the sleek and beautiful jet. The take-off was unreal after the long, laboured run of propeller-driven aircraft. We simply zoomed straight up into the sky in near silence. The plane only had half a dozen seats as it wasn't yet in service. I was invited to the co-pilot's seat, and for the first time was able to see the curvature of the earth from 40,000 feet. It took only a couple of hours to London instead of the usual five or six, and I took home strawberries bought in the Lebanon that morning. In those days such a thing was astonishing. Today's availability of almost anything almost any time from anywhere doesn't carry the thrill, the novelty of earlier times.

The fifties were an eventful decade for me; and one in which I suppose I made my reputation, such as it was, in the advertising world. I'd been a bit unwell after my South American trip (and I'm not talking about the Chilean oysters) and so, before undertaking another long trip to the Far East I thought I'd better consult Dr Walters, the Chest Physician who'd always looked after me. Happily, he wrote in January 1954 to say that he saw no reason for any recurrence; adding 'PS I really think you ought to have your personal chest physician travelling with you!'

Before I reached Tokyo, I stayed briefly in Manila. I watched some professionals playing Jai Alai – a skilful but dangerous-looking game. I also remember the intense heat and humidity. Leaving the frigid air conditioned hotel, you stepped into what seemed like an oven and were almost immediately drained of energy. The only place which beat even Manila was Aden, where you couldn't get dry even after a shower. (But I loved the little lizards which ran up and down the bathroom wall.) In Tokyo I stayed at the Imperial Hotel, designed by Frank Lloyd-Wright to be earthquake proof, and considered to be his finest work. It was demolished in 1968.

My main Japanese contact was Willie Something (can't remember what). His father was English and his mother was Japanese which, of course made him bilingual and an expert guide. Here I first sampled the rice wine Sake – and found I could drink a good deal of it and remain fairly sober – and the

An official BOAC photo: the caption reads 'Jack Swaab, Overseas Manager, Foote, Cone & Belding Ltd., London, arrives in Tokyo via BRITISH OVERSEAS AIRWAYS CORPORATION plane to study advertising and publicity of BOAC in Japan on his one-week stay here'.

raw fish which I didn't like as much as Dutch raw herring. Willie took me by train to the little seaside town of Hakone. On the way we passed Japan's highest mountain, Fujiyama, whose perfect shape glimmered serenely in the morning sunshine. It was one of those things you always hope to see before you die – like Naples. In the hotel in Hakone, we lived Japanese style, even exchanging my European clothes. We slept on the floor in rooms enclosed by thin (paper?) walls. I had some doubts about the nature of our hotel, when bidden to the communal bath I found that it was occupied by a number of lissom young Japanese girls. Before I could enter the water, one of these young ladies soaped me and poured a wooden bucket of warm water over me. The bath was blissfully warm, the girls laughed and chattered; not exactly like life in Wimbledon. It was a very pleasant evening. Don't ask. Willie took me to see the enormous 42-foot Daibutsu at Kamakura and along the totally urban road to Yokohama and I was fascinated by everything.

By contrast, a visit to Khartoum was less enjoyable. This was in 1956, when I had a recurrence, though only slight, of my TB. The estimable Dr

Walters allowed me to travel – with a large supply of INAH to be taken daily. There were delays along the way and I arrived at 2 in the morning. Our bus bumped across the moonlit desert road and dumped me together with another passenger at our rather seedy hotel. An unenthusiastic male receptionist informed me that I was to share a room with my sinister and unappetising fellow traveller. My furious – and actually rather impressive – outburst made it clear that having booked a single room, a single room was what I was going to have. And, eventually, sure enough at about 4 o'clock I fell into bed in what was apparently a prison cell. But it was *my* prison cell! Khartoum was very, very hot. You had to be careful opening the handle of a car door. You really could fry an egg on the pavement. I was shown a house where they were making meringues in a room under the roof and out of the sun. The heat was just right for cooking.

Although I didn't really enjoy my stay there (though I actually was able to top up my INAH at a local pharmacy), there was something special about walking along the palm tree-lined banks of the Nile. You had a sense of the centuries in which this, one of world's great rivers, had given life to so much of far-flung Africa.

Then there was India. The little I saw – Bombay, Calcutta, Delhi – left me with an ambition (never to be realised) to take a proper journey to the unvisited places. As it was, my recollections are mundane. At lunch by a swimming pool in Calcutta a kite swooped down, its wings brushing my hair as it stole the bread roll from my plate. Like most tourists, I was surprised to see cows ambling around the main shopping centre. I stayed at the Taj Mahal Hotel, the recent target of a terrorist attack. I must have left my wallet in my room when I went to breakfast one morning because when I returned to England, I found that some ingenious person had not only removed the English fivers but left the top one in place with plain paper 'notes' beneath. I was a bit more careful after that. To give you an idea of how times have changed: in Karachi, furious that my suitcase had not reached my hotel, I stomped off to the airport, found my Constellation plane, climbed up into the baggage compartment, found the case, summoned help, and had it delivered. I suppose the wartime habit of giving orders hadn't completely worn off. I think it was about that time that there was clamour from the Greek community in Cyprus, and from Greece, for Enosis – union of Greece and Cyprus, a longstanding grievance like Argentina and the Falklands, Gibraltar, Ulster and other heritages of our imperial past. Voice was given to Enosis by the turbulent priest Archbishop Makarios. I used to see him holding court in the GB – the Grand Bretagne Hotel – Athens at teatime.

Those early, demanding, work-filled days of long-haul travel involved my life in an unfamiliar, exciting regime: the big new aircraft – Constellation, DC6, Coronado, Britannia – with their throbbing rush, on take-off from faraway airports. Putting faces to the letterheads in my office. The food – especially in the Orient – and the unfamiliar smells and sounds. And, of course, the chance to see things and places hitherto only names in a book: The Little Mermaid in Copenhagen, the Imperial Palace in Vienna, the Daibatsu at Kamakura. I had my shirts made for a song in Hong Kong and became rather demanding at expensive hotels! And in 1958 something very important happened: the arrival of our second son, Peter who – perhaps because of Zena's Canadian habit of nicknaming everyone – has always been called Pete. Zena was forty-three when he arrived (by Caesarean like his brother) and it was just as well that we didn't fully realise the risks at that age. In fact, I was pretty relaxed about Pete, whereas in Richard's case I was racked with anxiety daily until Zena emerged safely from the bathroom in the morning; and I lost seven pounds in a couple of weeks after he arrived. Things were very different from my childhood. As a Canadian, Zena would never have contemplated sending our boys to boarding school. It didn't take me long to agree with her, but we were lucky in having KCS Wimbledon, a highly rated day school, just across the road and in due course they both got scholarships there and, later, to Cambridge.

Something else which was important also happened that year. In November, I was invited to become General Manager of CPV International, part of Colman, Prentis and Varley, a well-known, if slightly eccentric Advertising Agency. My headhunter was Leslie Cort, one of the small band of overseas executives such as Henry Deschampneufs, Geoffrey Meadmore, John Reed and myself who were achieving some expertise in the field. I still have cuttings of articles I wrote on the subject of worldwide advertising and its pitfalls, to *Advertisers' Weekly*. I'd made many friends in different parts of the world who had welcomed me back after TB. Fifty-eight now wrote warmly on my departure from FCB.

I was to taste heady success at CPV International where I became Joint Managing Director; but disaster (and treachery) struck, and like Mammon in *Paradise Lost*, I 'with the setting sun / Dropt from the zenith like a falling star'. However, all that was in the future when I was first taken in to receive Varley's approval. I'm not sure whether he was drunk or just quixotic that morning, but he was so unpleasant that on leaving I told Leslie that not only could I not consider working for him but I couldn't see why anyone else did. I was persuaded to change my mind. With my early successes, Varley

Zena, Roie, Peter and
Richard, Cornwall
1960.

smiled upon me. Zena and I were invited to eat grouse at his flat in Mount Street, and with the boys when we were on holiday in Cornwall we were invited to his beautiful house in Devon. We met his charming wife Elizabeth (Montagu) and his delightful younger daughter Martha (with whom I next corresponded in 2009). We were greeted with an enormous vat of Black Velvet; Varley never did things by halves. He always insisted on being addressed by his surname. When we went for a stroll by the river after lunch, Richard said to him, 'Varley, you must be very rich.' 'Why so?' 'Well, all that ginger beer at lunch, and the strawberries growing here.' By February 1960 things were going well at CPVI and I was made a Director.

But I never quite shook off the faint unease I felt when I joined CPV just before Christmas 1958. Varley, I always felt, had the vaguely but ominously noble features of a Roman Emperor, and the ambience was, indeed, reminiscent of Caesar's Senate in January 44 BC. If, as was generally supposed, Varley's policy was based on *Divide et Impera*, he was successful enough. Led by Cyrus Ducker, formerly of Patrick Dolan's new agency, the conspirators simmered with rebellion. Cyrus told me, 'you're going to have to decide whom to back'. The most able among them was John Pearce. I attended several of his brilliant presentations and it was no surprise when he left to form his own Agency. He wanted to give me a job when I left

CPV, but was overruled by the rest of his Directors. I never met Prentis, ex-Crawfords who founded CPV in 1934, but I was on good terms with Bob Colman who shared my horse-racing addiction. I think that about all Bob could have brought to the Agency was money from the mustard connection, because he wasn't very bright. He had the good fortune to expire in his armchair watching the racing one Saturday afternoon. A last photo-finish perhaps? Maybe I'm being unfair to Drummond Armstrong, one-time Director of the IPA, but I always regarded him as the Lepidus figure around the court; a role, incidentally, perfectly suited more recently to the insidious Jack Straw. Then there was Terence Clarke MP, an ex-Brigadier and, it was said, Varley's CO at some point. I usually encountered him in the Directors' dining room. As he said, 'I've nothing against Jews, I'm just glad I'm not one'. 'So am I', I remarked to my neighbour. Just as well Terry didn't hear me as he was very large and said to be an army boxing champion. He drank quite a lot and gambled heavily. In spite of his 'tolerant' attitude to Jews and his well publicised anti-Communist outbursts, I happened to know that he was involved in some very dubious dealings originating behind the Iron Curtain with both of the above. I couldn't blow the whistle on him because I had to protect my source. I enjoyed seeing what a furiously bad loser he was when he was defeated at a general election. Nor must I overlook Leslie Cort, angler with the job at CPVI as his bait, and nicknamed The Bishop because of his unctuous parsonic speech. Although affecting a rather lofty attitude he betrayed his (I think) fairly humble origins by tremendous obsequiousness to those he regarded as his superiors: Lord Geddes for example, my Client at the British Travel Association, whom he addressed as 'My Lord'. But I almost had to admire the hypocritical zest with which he consumed a pint of Guinness when we were pitching for one of their South American brands.

CPV was a place of legend. Before my time, I was told, a certain senior executive used to walk around with a leopard, or some similar jungle cat, on a lead. And in my time one of the fellow diners in the Directors' dining-room was a terrifying Mrs Spencer-Phillips, who clearly dismissed me as white trash. I never quite understood what she did and assumed that, like some others, she was a relic of Varley's past. A number of us disreputable ad men have written fact or fiction based on our business and given no more than a taste of the lurid scene at CPV it is easy to see why. And suddenly I realise that I have omitted John Maples, an eminent figure in financial circles, and the *Deus ex Machina* of the entire organisation. He is the only person whom I have what they now call 'blanked'. After engineering my downfall, he came up to me, all smiles and outstretched hand at some advertising function. A kind of paralysis made me unable to do anything but look straight through him. He was shocked. All this, of course, relates to CPV at 34 Grosvenor Street, but I was at CPV International or CPVI at 43 Park Street, five minutes away. I was not unknown to several of my new staff, because the international advertising world was still fairly small and I had become fairly well known within it. Moreover, by chance, the creative director had been at my niece Monica's wedding a week or two before and had been impressed by the quite funny speech I had made. Like John the Baptist, he had gone before me, spreading expectation of the wit to come. This was George Frost, who merited the nickname of Mr Toad by his ebullient driving of the Rolls-Royces he loved to collect. A founder of the Twenty Ghost Club, he later bought a Phantom II – distinguished by a bible rack put to good use no doubt by its previous owner, Cardinal Griffin.

From my first day, I realised that my new job at CPVI would be much more demanding – and enjoyable – than the one I had left. Now I would be responsible for the Agency's creative output, for going after new business and for hiring (and maybe firing) staff, which then numbered three or four dozen but later grew to over seventy. And it was at this time that the Balkwill family entered the life of my own family.

This is how. I had taken on a pleasant lady approaching middle age as a temporary secretary for one of the Directors. One morning I was telling someone about a horse I was thinking of backing that day at Newbury. 'I wouldn't advise it, he's much better on a right handed course.' What magic was this? None other than 'Mrs B' – Bridget my betting partner and friend thereafter. We had some sensational betting coups together, notably when we got the Daily Tote Treble at Royal Ascot. Bridget occasionally would say, 'I took the liberty of putting ten bob for you on so and so today'. She was a good selector; and her husband Michael was knowledgeable too. Bridget coined a phrase after she'd changed her mind about a winner and failed to back it. 'I gave an animal howl!' Thereafter we did what I called, 'betting against the howl', ie preferring to back a loser than missing a winner through last-minute mind changes. Pete – who is an adventurous (and largely successful) punter – and I still use the phrase.

I visited Bridget on her deathbed the day before she died. Her poor once-chubby cheeks were skeletal, ravaged by cancer as she lay in her sunny, flower-laden room. As I leave she says in a loud clear voice, 'Goodbye Jack'. But all that was in the future. Mrs B introduced us all to her family, living then at Cobham. Michael was in the upper echelons of the BBC, and responsible among other things for organising the General Election night

This page:
The Balkwills, 1967.
Richard Balkwill,
Richard and Peter
Swaab, Philip Balkwill;
Bridget and Michael
Balkwill.

TV broadcast and writing a history of the BBC. A brilliant, modest man, he had won the Newdigate poetry prize at Oxford. They had two sons. Philip, the elder, dazzling, charismatic was an inspired schoolteacher at Charterhouse. Richard, the younger, was never called anything but Pouncer and is still to this very day. I sometimes phone him for publishing guidance as he has had an impressive career in the business. What wonderful days we had, playing fiendish card games ferociously contended at Cobham and later, when Michael and Bridget moved to Century Cottage in Semley near Shaftesbury, Twizzle and Win-a-lot. Mistakes were related to racing: cries of 'fell at last', 'stumbled on landing', 'ran on under pressure'. All this was immortalised in a little book produced by Pete, called *The Acrimony Book* which describes 'all the results of Twizzle and Win-a-Lot after the New Year of 1969'. He meticulously records who was winning most, highest scores etc with notes such as 'particularly spiteful and acrimonious', 'Dad was very slow and played rather badly', 'Chairman was very strict, extremely spiteful game', 'Excellent banking by Peter who got low record', 'B says to M, "I thought you went first last time." M says coolly, "Well, you were wrong".' I treasure the *Acrimony Book*.

Philip married a delightful person called Lesley – or usually to all of us, Lez. She and Elisabeth, Pouncer's wife, and all of them used to stay with us at Pilots, the house in Porthcothan Bay, near Padstow, which we rented some seventy times from 1956 on. On the way back, setting off before dawn, we'd call at Century for breakfast. The last, downhill stretch was always called the Assyrian Hill (as in Byron's poem 'The Assyrian came down like a wolf on the fold ....'), and our arrival was known as The Semley Express.

Alas, Philip died, ridiculously young, in 1997. He had an impressive obituary in the *Daily Telegraph*. Bridget told me the delightful story of his first day at school, when, returning tearfully, he asked if he could look at the 'Cyclosopedia'.

1959 saw the start of the most – what can I call them? – dramatic years of my life as an ad man. Or, since I am writing in 2012, perhaps I should say Mad Men as I spent time with our American partner, Kenyon & Eckhardt, in that infamous thoroughfare. On visits I used to take the helicopter from the airport to downtown Manhattan, where it landed on the roof of the Pan Am building. (Looking down at the steel-clad cavernous streets, I tried not to think what engine failure might entail. I believe in later years some such disaster with a rotor did occur, and the service was discontinued.)

By 1961, the Agency had collected sixteen new accounts and the one which gave me the most pride was the GNTO, the National Tourist Organisation

Jack and Greek colleagues at the
Parthenon, 1953.

of Greece. I had first secured this account when I was at FCB, and we ran
a short, modest campaign based on 'Greece, Land of Myth and Magic'. I
don't think it generated very magical tourist figures. In 1959 I heard from
my good friend and Greek Agency contact, Chris Papadopoulos, that the
account might be available again. I flew to Athens and took part in some
negotiations which, I felt, could only be written up for the CPV board in the
style of an Eric Ambler thriller, maybe as 'Events in the House at 87 Kythinos
Street'. Anyway, we got the business; I opened a small office in Athens and
set about devising a campaign. I have to take personal credit for this. I
laboured over a weekend filling pieces of paper and at last came up with
four potent words: Greece Greets You Warmly. Like Mr Blandings who built
his dream house, also an ad man, who made his name with four immortal
words about a laxative. Finally, taking a real risk, our campaign featured
some of the modern attractions – sea, sand, sun, wine and (only implied)
sex. We were greatly helped by the inspired idea of George Frost, our Art
Director, to employ the famous (fashion) photographer, Norman Parkinson,
who toured for several weeks and brought back some unforgettable images.

When I presented the campaign in Athens, the management was stunned, and took a good deal of convincing. I was helped by their manager, Theophilos Frangopoulous (always called Bulis or Bulaki – a diminutive favoured by the Greeks). Bulis came to London and told the CPV board that I was the most astute negotiator they'd ever encountered! As I explained (after he'd left the meeting) this should be translated as their taking my habit of telling the truth as the ultimate in devious behaviour. (No wonder Troy fell.) I was listening to the radio the night the Greeks threw out the Colonels, and I'm sure that one of the passionate interviewees was Bulis. The Greek campaign took wings; tourist figures boomed to the first million. I was made a Director of CPV and later Joint Managing Director. Bill Shelton, the successful manager of CPV Colombiana, joined as a Director. Also promoted was Ian Harvey, a former Foreign Office minister I'd known at FCB and found rather overbearing and conceited. His political career came to an abrupt halt after some homosexual scandal in Green Park. Maybe it was 'sweet are the uses of adversity' or something, but Ian became much less pompous and much more approachable. We now became quite good friends. He invited Zena and me to dinner with him and his wife, Claire. It wasn't long after Ian's downfall and the atmosphere was painfully tense. Zena liked to relate one of my most celebrated *faux pas*. I had been abroad and calling a staff meeting on my return, explained that I'd been quite relaxed, 'as Ian was keeping my seat warm for me'. I think he was mildly amused. I felt a hot flush wash over me.

I made a further inspired move when I assigned a beautiful young copywriter to the account. Shelagh Brookesmith as she then was (and later, as Shelagh Macdonald, a successful author) wrote some brilliant campaigns in the ensuing years, spending time in the country and becoming fluent in Greek. She built a home – reachable only by sea or donkey – on the island of Serifos. I had to fire our first Athens manager and replace him with an enterprising if slightly dodgy young Scot called Murray Smith. He drove in the Acropolis Rally, coming fourth, and I have to admit that being a passenger in his Mini was one of the more frightening experiences of my thirteen visits to Greece. Murray flourished and ended up rather successfully in New York. He had a darling French wife with an enchanting accent, but their marriage didn't survive. (He was reputed to have snorkelled up some rather illegal treasures from the sea bed but, if so, escaped any consequences.) In 1966 we won the Golden Tulip of the International Advertising Association, for Europe's best advertising campaign. I went to Stockholm for the presentation to our client who, breaking with normal tradition, failed to mention the Agency's part in this success – achieved in the face of their reluctant acceptance. I took to this occasion one of my Directors, Geoffrey Kean. He was fat and reminded me of Oscar Ashe, a portly actor I had seen as a twelve-year-old in *Julius Caesar* at His Majesty's Theatre, portraying 'damnèd Casca' who 'like a cur, struck Caesar in the neck'. I found out later that Geoffrey, whom I had promoted, had plotted incessantly against me; and thereafter, always thought of him as 'damnèd Casca'. I think he ended up running a rather suspect mail order company. The GNTO presented Zena and me with a visit to Greece. We took the 'classical tour' of the Peloponnese and spent a magical moment at Olympia standing on the 200 metres of the original Olympic Games, the silence broken only by a melodious cowbell. We were stuck in the lift in our hotel at Epidauros, where an event occurred which Zena felt merited inclusion in a phrasebook: 'Excuse me, your tortoise has sauntered across our balcony'.

If the Greek account had a romantic element, the Imperial Automatic Washing Machine one was entirely practical. There were other such machines but this was the first we attempted to sell direct to the customer via couponed advertisements. It was also very testing. There was a precise daily pattern of responses; and immediate evidence of an unsuccessful ad. The campaign was headed by a hard-headed and clever young chief copywriter called Drayton Bird. I still remember the plaintive weekly demand of the client's wife, 'Where are the new *ideas*, Mr Swaab?' which tested Drayton's ingenuity – and stamina. And mine. Leslie Cort saw some personal mileage in all this and helped to construct what was seen as a respectable Board of Directors for Imperial. Foremost was an old friend of his, the onetime sprinter Elaine Burton, now Baroness Burton. With her was always her Mouse, rather like Dame Edna's Madge. Nobody asked any awkward questions. Then there was Bernard Rickatson-Hatt (you couldn't make it up), a well known financial PR figure. There was Leslie. There was Abraham Seltzer, the managing director. His wife Amy, the incessant Idea Hunter. And, I think, Mr Rader, the solicitor. The Directors were all handsomely rewarded, but when Abe (known in city circles as Alka Seltzer) committed suicide and the company crashed (injudicious borrowing and lending), they speedily took to the hills. I liked Abe and was sorry about his sad end. The Imperial – made in Italy – was a damn good machine. I used one (a Christmas gift from Mr S) for twenty-four years.

The things that come back to me .... How Bruce Fox the Managing Director of Glacier Mints said to me in the middle of a meeting about a new ad campaign, '*He* wouldn't like these' –pointing to the ceiling. Bruce meant his long dead father who had invented this rather sickly sweet. Bruce wouldn't accept my suggestion that he should market the mints in a small tube (like Spangles). Maybe *he* approved after all because years later that's just what I saw.

CPVI was now also beginning to operate in the UK – and successfully. People were heard to say that it was the most go-ahead part of the organisation. Perhaps pride (my pride) went before the fall which was still a year or two in the future. But I think it was mostly due to misjudgement of clients who let me down, and colleagues who not only failed to support but also made fatal errors which I should have spotted or corrected, but didn't.

An important account win was British European Airways, struggling with an inferiority complex over BOAC and represented by their Advertising Manager, John Burkhart, whose undoubted efficiency and ability, marred by an unpleasant and bullying attitude, made him widely detested by the Agency. As it happens, I didn't seem included in the bullying. With a big effort, I got on with him, aided by regular dinners at a place in Wimpole Street which served the steak tartare which he liked. As you might guess, Varley did not endear himself to this Client, and when we lost BEA John told me (over a mouthful of steak tartare), 'It's only due to you that you didn't lose the account a year ago'. Varley also lost me the British Travel Association account, when, somewhat worse for alcoholic wear, he persisted throughout a meeting in yelling at Lord Geddes, 'Point of order, point of order'.

But my most important Client was BAT – British American Tobacco, which also became my subsequent employer. I'm pretty sure – I never went out of my way to find out – that this was mainly due to an unlikely friendship with the chairman, Sir Richard Dobson. An ex-Cambridge scholar, ex-Spitfire pilot, he had a razor sharp mind, a reputation for not suffering fools gladly; and was deeply respected – and feared! In a long profile in *The Times* in 1976, he summed up his approach to business and people as:

I think what people really value in a leader is the professional who is likely to get it right. It is no good having a hero who leads you into battle and you immediately get killed, however, gloriously.

There are two kinds of people. One kind who secures a problem like a bone and puts it down at your feet. The other kind says, 'here is a problem. I think this is the way we should deal with it'. There is quite a sharp distinction between those two people and I prefer the latter. It is quite easy to cut people down to size but it is almost impossible to blow them up to size if it comes to that sort of thing.

I had, of course, made several presentations to BAT and incidentally discovered that we shared a taste for violent thrillers which we exchanged. But not many people know that Richard was also a sensitive person – and a poet. I have his fine poem *Burma 1944* given to me by his wife Betty. To me it has always carried echoes of Newbolt's, 'He fell among thieves'. He was – like most people – captivated by Zena's charm when we were invited to dinner at his large, comfortable house in Richmond. We got to know it well with lunches and competitive bridge; and became friends with him and Betty. They have both died, Betty on a day we were to lunch together, and I miss them. But these days I often feel like T. S. Eliot's Tiresias, 'sat by Thebes below the wall', saddened by all that's happened, and is to come.

You won't, I think, (especially in today's climate) want details of our cigarette campaigns. However, I do take a certain perverse pride in one for State Express 555 which was selected by the powers that be as exemplifying exactly the sort of thing which would not be permitted on TV.

I've almost forgotten that it was during this, my most successful time, probably late in 1963 or 1964 that I was struck by the first of the two bouts of clinical depression I have undergone. I think it may have been triggered by what I thought was my heart missing a beat; though, in fact, it was putting in an extra one – an extra systole. Or maybe it was the stressful long hours; or the drinks cabinet in my office. Whatever; I retired to bed, couldn't eat, thought about ways of ending it all. A classic case. And I was so lucky. One spring morning I woke up and it had all gone. I had a good breakfast. I felt optimistic, ready to face the future. I say I was so lucky because there seemed to be no reason that I could find for the black dog's departure.

Just as well, because the storm clouds were just over the horizon. We lost BEA, we lost BTA; but we did gain Canadian Pacific Airlines which gave me the opportunity to revisit Vancouver, Zena's hometown. I suppose it was the one account I would have chosen to win; and they did give Zena and me a first class return ticket. What a family reunion that was! But, as I say, storm clouds.

The Greeks, feeling that they were less reliant on us now, became difficult. Their late payments which had always been dilatory now started damaging our cash flow. The loss of Imperial left a big gap. But worst, a couple of accounts whose names I can't even recall, but about which I had doubts, had been ushered in by Bill Shelton and damnèd Casca, and began to miss payments; and finally, weren't going to make any payments. A cash crisis arose and I was elected as scapegoat. I wrote earlier that Bill had let me down. It was now, in my hour of need, that he equivocated and deserted.

Leslie wasn't going to jeopardise his position – Joint Managing Director but not very joint at this moment. Varley said he'd always had doubts about my appointment! I was too tired to fight. I resigned. My staff was horrified but unable to influence the course of events. Especially sad was 'Wilkie' my little handyman, bless him, who at one of our Christmas parties had proposed a toast to 'our wonderful guv'nor'.

It was a sad end to the best years of my advertising life. My two small boys were worried, though I assured them (without much evidence) that all would be well. I received much sympathy but tangible help came from Mervyn, veteran of many shared Cornish summers, and by now my best friend. He organised a well-paid job for me at a new Anglo-American Agency called PKG–Brunning. There were only four of us: Geoff Goodyear whom I'd known for years but who was no sort of soulmate; his secretary; myself and my loyal PA Kathryn Nairn (to whom I'd given her first job), who had left with me. After the unlamented demise of PKG-B, she went on to great success as a Director of Ogilvy & Mather. (Sort of fitting in the scheme of things; Kathryn gave Richard his first job; and, like her, he has gone on to breathe the thin air.) I was truly unhappy at PKG-B. The Brunnings part was located in a rather scruffy East End building. The people seemed (maybe unfairly) very second-rate; and finally the Americans (who, I think, secretly shared my opinion) closed the West End bit (PKG) and fired us with a month's notice. Apart from not having a salary, I really didn't care!

CHAPTER 10

1968-79. A DECADE AT B.A.T. CORNWALL

Following my PKG quietus, undeserved but unlamented, Mervyn and I decided to take a holiday at the house in Cornwall which we'd discovered ten years before. This house – Pilots – and this place – Porthcothan Bay have played such a large part in the lives of our two families, that I must tell you about them. Zena and I went to St Minver in the summer of 1954 and although we resisted a Beckham-type naming, May 1955 made it clear that Richard had his origins in the West Country. Next year, Mervyn and I, Zena and Patricia, Mervyn's wife, set out for our destination, a farm at St Columb, with Richard and Patrick our two children. We were in my willing but limited A40 heavily loaded and topped by a roof rack on which were roped a cot and sundry cases. Our next journey was undertaken in Mervyn's much superior company Zodiac, the rope superseded by a heavy elastic thing. As we sailed down the A3 with cries of 'Thrummers West!', a wheel trim sailed noisily off. Thrummers was the sound of rope or elastic hitting the roof. The farm was Starkadder Country, straight from *Cold Comfort Farm*. The three or four hundred flies in the bedrooms called for an early visit to the chemist. The family ate their meals in trousers and vests, our food was plain but plentiful – specially the potatoes – and pigs propagated noisily under our windows at dawn. In the hall, a large stuffed owl glared angrily under a glass case. She closely resembled our hostess and we always called her Mrs R. However, it was here that we discovered 'Pilots'. Each day we motored five miles from St Columb towards Padstow, and on one such journey, we noticed a road sign on a wall reading 'Porthcothan ¼ mile'. I say 'we noticed' as both Mervyn and I have claimed to have seen it, and because over the years each is more certain he was the one, it is better not to pursue the dispute in these pages. We found Porthcothan, a long narrow beach of smooth sand, blessed with splendid surf. And there, parked on the stony entrance to the beach, we bathed each day.

Porthcothan Bay, Cornwall.

On one side of the bay no houses but the coastal path which crossed the beach. On the other side, a small road with a few houses and we liked the look of one – Pilots – and wondered if it was to let. I went in (there was no-one there), had a quick look around, reported back and discovered from the local agents, Button, Menhennet & Mutton (the Cornish Mafia round whom we imagined a web of scurrilous activities) the name of the owner, Mrs Robinson, alas now dead. We were by now rather disenchanted with the amorous pigs and the frequent rain (Cornwall can be like that) and next year Pilots was ours; the first of over seventy visits. It was a perfect holiday place, and over the years its history, its traditions, its very vocabulary became part of our two families' memories.

In those days, we went into uncluttered Padstow for morning coffee at Bill's, where the entire large tin of biscuits was left on the table. Or to Keith Barnicutts (known as Barney's) with their succulent (cholesterol-laden) doughnuts. 'Barneycutians', Mervyn would sing, 'they're the jammiest cakes you saw. When you've had one you want more'. His father was Director of Music, Royal Marines Chatham and Mervyn was very musical. We had an introduction to the Prideaux-Brune family at Prideaux Place. Zena asked if there was plenty of running space for the boys. There was: a deer park, of, I think, 5,000 acres.

Back at Porthcothan we sat as though in the theatre stalls, watching Wills Rock as it rose like some enormous submarine conning tower by the headland. The huge Atlantic rollers crashed over it with what we called Wills Thunderers Mark I, II or III or – inspirationally by Phil Balkwill, the 'Wedding Veil' – self-explanatory. At the occasional very low tide you could scramble on to Wills Rock. We were so glad we didn't know that the boys had climbed it until after the event. We hired surfboards from the little shop by the beach and this activity also had its own language: 'board buck' when the surf was choppy; 'beach grounders' for perfect landward runs. There was the 'Mummy Farm' where we bought clotted cream; Mr Percy Keast the butcher in St Merryn who had the best legs of lamb in the world (and loins of pork), which we ate to the bone at a sitting. Nor must I forget in later years Captain Beaky, the arrogant seagull who rapped on my window as each day broke. There was cricket in the garden, with the annual award of 'catch of the holiday' (won so memorably one year at mid-off by Carey). We hired a little black and white TV (later the house had a colour set of its own) to enable us to follow the horses at the Padstow bookie. The most notable bet was twenty-year-old Pete's yankee – a combination of four horses in eleven bets. His outlay of just over a pound won him well over two hundred. As the years went by, Porthcothan's charm never faded. Carey and Alan visited on their honeymoon, things became less rudimentary, the beach shop was almost mini-Fortnums in its stock selection. We loved it all but occasionally looked a bit wistfully back to Mr Strongman's tin of tongue, which he tried in vain to sell to us over, it seems, years. Then there were local characters, some of whom we veterans got to know: 'The Lady', a judge's widow who though elderly bathed each day and 'The Lady' in the newsagents in Padstow, who winked. Involuntarily, we realised – just in time. Mrs J. and her white bikini … The Kelly's ice-cream van with its melodious chimes as it arrived on the beach each day. Overflowing cones were brought back to Pilots. The ancient boiler which gave rise to alarming clonking in the night and the need to run off the boiling brown water, was replaced by one which may have lacked a bit of character but was a pleasure to service.

Next, however, came a grim time with apparently hopeful job interviews leading to nothing. I didn't enjoy going for the dole every week (even if the notes were usually crisp and new).

Four increasingly stressful months passed. It was a bad time for Zena. Then one day came a call out of the blue from Richard Haddon, the BAT Advertising Manager. They had a project which would give me temporary work with future possibilities. That was in November 1967. In 1968 I was offered a full time job at BAT; probably the only person not taken on through the usual channels.

Most ad men subscribe to the truism that it, 'would be a great business without the Clients'. And here I was, after all these defamatory years: a Client! Mind you, as cogs go in the various wheels, I would have fitted inside a watch movement; but it felt good: somewhere to work, a salary, even a (small) pension to look forward to. And no more visits to the Job Centre. There was something faintly imperial about BAT. Vaguely anonymous old men, it seemed, sat in the numerous small rooms doing nobody knew what – but they had probably also done it in Tientsin or Tierra del Fuego in the days gone by. The Directors – august and remote – moved in splendour on The Third Floor (it was referred to in capitals) – richly panelled, deeply carpeted and watched over benignly by the portraits of past chairmen. I had only been there once in earlier times when Zena and I were invited to a buffet occasion of such richness that she nearly passed out on one of the opulent sofas.

Yes, BAT was a benign dictatorship. Marriage to the natives was discouraged – especially before the war but there was also a good (free) canteen. A nurse was on hand for minor ailments and 'flu injections (also free). A well-stocked shop sold goods from various BAT companies such as Yardley at competitive prices. When there were energy strikes, BAT had its own generators to provide heating. Two further benefits from an apparently old-fashioned company were the introduction of flex-time working and an inflation-based salary increase each year. You didn't have to be a smoker, but if you were, there was a weekly ration – in my case 100 cigarettes.

When I joined the advertising department, we were fairly recent entrants to a world which called for competitive activity as opposed to the many years of benevolent supply to a backward world's demand. At the same time, the first, increasingly aggressive anti-smoking organisations were forcing restrictions on what could be said – and where and when – about the alleged pleasures of our product. It's amazing to remember that in the UK back in 1960, a pack of twenty cigarettes cost 20p. Today I was behind a man in Sainsbury's whose purchase of 8 packs rang up £48.00 on the till. It took me back to our occupation of Germany when the war ended. Cigarettes could get you anything from a bottle of schnapps to a *cinq à sept*.

Saint-Paul-de-Vence.

The tempo of life compared to an Ad Agency could only be described as leisurely. The advertising manager, to whom I had reported, was middle-aged and had obviously been overtaken by events. Luckily for him, his assistant, Richard Haddon, was an energetic and intelligent young man who had succeeded him and who, officially at least, hired me. One of Richard's best commercials was a *James Bond* spoof. It featured the really dazzling Joanna Lumley whose menacing automatic turned out to be a cigarette lighter.

We had always got on well. I think I was reasonably useful to him as I'd handled all the BAT business in my previous life. He sent me on some overseas jobs, memorably one which entailed staying at La Colombe d'Or in Saint-Paul-de-Vence, a magical village in Provence – which enchanted me as we filmed in the Ardèche gorge by the trout-filled river and had coffee and cheese in the square at Aix. The hotel, was, in effect a museum of modern art worth millions. The original owner had often been paid in paintings so that your bedroom wall probably had a couple of Dufys or some Impressionists. I had the good fortune to have a chat with James Baldwin who knew my literary agent cousin in New York. What a privilege to talk to the author of *The Fire Next Time* and some seriously good novels, which happily I'd read. He was a funny, ugly little man of overwhelming charm. Meeting him was a very high spot of my increasing years. Another high spot of a rather different kind was during a shoot in Palma. I can't remember a thing about the commercial itself but I do remember hiring a car and going to a club called Sergeant Pepper's Lonely Hearts. There, stunned by the appalling music, the strobe lights and the tribal dance and chanting of the (very young) clientele, I consumed an ill-advisedly large portion of a bottle of vodka; I, who have no head for alcohol. Emerging fuddled in the small hours I actually drove through unknown streets back to my hotel. I *backed* into a parking space, reached my room and swooned into the darkness. Next day I had the worst hangover since, well I couldn't remember since when. Another less disgraceful expedition was to Holland. This involved organising the rotation of windmill sails (shades of 1944) and opening of canal bridges. It was good to be back in Holland and locate some raw herring for lunch.

The years passed and as my contribution grew slightly less minuscule I was allowed to use the company dining-room to entertain Agency people (reversing my own earlier experience) and other suppliers. We still saw something of the Dobsons and one of my duties was to mark his card at Royal Ascot, where he was always in one of the boxes. Happily – and surprisingly, considering the usual doom-laden punters at this meeting – I usually managed to find him a few winners; indeed, one year he won the sweepstake run by his, no doubt, illustrious companions. In 1977, addressing a small private meeting of retailers, he made a cavalier and indiscreet reference to 'wogs'. Unfortunately his speech was secretly tape-recorded by the son of one of the guests, the remark (which he always insisted had been quoted out of context) was leaked by the press and amid much righteous indication, he was forced to resign. As I told him at lunch soon after, it was our loss not his. Richard's successor was Patrick (later Sir Patrick) Sheehy, the Marketing Director.

Sheehy had the reputation of being a bit of a Rottweiler and I must admit that I found him rather alarming at meetings I attended. However, I do recall that at one such meeting he did surprise me by referring to me as, 'that wise old owl'. Wise, *moi*? BAT had a rule that called for retirement at sixty-one, which I would reach in 1979. As I worked on in two other, quite different jobs until I was seventy-five this was disappointing – and cost me a lot of money after shares were made available to all staff the year after I left. A year or two before then, there was a major re-organisation of

Marketing and Advertising and I was made Advertising Services Manager which sounded a lot more important than it was. I think it was probably a rather BAT way of not kicking me out with only a short time left before I had to go anyway. Actually the job was quite interesting. I was given some of the small brands and left to devise my own advertising campaigns, using all media and employing various small freelance companies. It was enjoyable to have such a free hand and I did produce one or two half-decent little campaigns. Perhaps the one of which I was most proud was for Broadway in the Caribbean. *Make a Hit with Broadway* appeared next to cricket scoreboards at Test matches throughout the West Indies. (Five more immortal words!)

BAT had thrown me a timely lifeline and now I left with a cardful of kind wishes (backed up to this day with a regular lunch at Wentworth) from some kind colleagues. There is a handsome Orrefors glass bowl (engraved with equine athletes) in my living room; and an illustrated testimonial on the wall in the downstairs loo bears testimony to my 'unique' BAT career.

CHAPTER 11

1979-94. RETIREMENT AND NEW CAREERS

But here I was in 1979: sixty-one years old, marbles reduced but functional and not enough money to live on. However, a third career beckoned. It so happened that the father of one of Richard's school friends owned a couple of bookshops. He and his wife – a friend of Zena's – lived nearby and we'd seen something of one another over the years. Now, nudged by his daughter, he was prevailed upon to offer me a job selling books. Thus I spent the next eight enjoyable years until the bookshop was sold. The Regency Bookshop in Esher was a dusty rambling place full of nooks and crannies; a sort of *Old Curiosity Shop*. And the Dickensian ambience was reinforced when I was introduced to the manager with such a Dickensian name: Robert Snuggs. We had a very old till with a loud bell, though this was duly replaced with a rather hard-to-operate electronic machine. I'd always enjoyed books, reading them, reading reviews etc. So I was reasonably well-informed. And I enjoyed serving customers, particularly those seeking advice and information. By the time the job ended I had a number of regulars who wouldn't go on holiday without my reading list.

The owner, Dr Michael Lancet, was a pre-war refugee from Vienna. I was never able to unravel the exact nature of his D.Phil, which had apparently been granted by Oxford University in one year, based on some previous unspecified work in Vienna. He had, rather shrewdly, published two books, *The History of Esher*, and *The History of Kingston*. They reprinted steadily and were cash cows for the shops. (The other one was in Surbiton.) His other passion was the Rotary Club. He became President (or whatever) of the local club and even got involved with Rotary International which called for time and travel. In this way I took over more and more and was the *de facto* Manager. The shop supplied the local library and several schools so there were several ladies involved with inserting labels, fastening plastic sleeves etc. as well as the ones selling in the shop.

When the Doctor was away, I also saw reps, ordered books and reorganised the layout, shelving, window displays and other minutiae. The Doctor had never felt it necessary to warm the shop and when I first arrived we had to work in overcoats and mittens. I crossed swords with him on this, even having to quote the figures in some industrial act or other, and in the end he allowed me to get some storage heaters installed and an electric fan (which he turned off when I wasn't around!) There remained for many years a sort of amiable warfare over this matter, but we managed to coexist. This was in large measure because I found the work so intensely interesting and enjoyable. This was especially true at Christmas where you had to judge what would be the bestsellers and how many to gamble on ordering. If you got that wrong you could find yourself lumbered with losers or unable to get stock when you needed it. On this, too, the Doctor and I didn't see eye to eye, as he had a deep rooted aversion to ordering in quantity whereas I, always a gambler I suppose, tended to take chances. But though I say it myself, I was rather good at my job and the shop did well. It was a real thrill to reach over £1,000 in one day at Christmas. One snag about the Dickensian character of the shop was that it readily lent itself to theft – often of the most audacious kind such as the removal of one large volume of the Shorter Oxford Dictionary and a week later, its Companion. (Dictionary corner was difficult to oversee.) The artbook section was also particularly vulnerable.

One day, three young West Indians – two men and a girl – came in about lunchtime. We were thin on the ground but I was happy to indulge (in the sports section) in nostalgic recollections of the four great Ws of past Windies teams with one of the men. The others browsed about the shop – in particular into Michael's office where they emptied the petty cash tin. I think this was only discovered after he returned from lunch. We did call the police, only to discover that this gang had claimed a number of local victims; none, I fear, more gullible than me, the cricket enthusiast.

I'm glad to see that local booksellers are still surviving. The essence of a good shop is still a knowledgeable and interested staff. True, where we had to use reference books, reviews and – above all our memories, today's booksellers can fall back on Google and other computer-borne aids.

As an author myself, I hate to see the Christmas windows filled with ghost-written celebrity bestsellers whose authors can sometimes not put together a sentence let alone a book. It amazes me how many copies of these books sell; especially when my own miserable royalty cheques arrive! I'm quite prepared to admit to being envious, but selling books like groceries doesn't

Giving a speech at Bé's 80th birthday party.

reflect too well on our society. But then, what does? Surely, being a bookseller must be one of today's few sources of job satisfaction. I still recall after the pleasure of serving some of my regulars who wouldn't go on holiday without my recommended list; or in some cases – especially the rich local ladies – who relied on me to select something for their wealthy husbands' Christmas stockings. I had always been under the impression that when Michael was going to sell the Esher shop, there would be a job for me at Surbiton. In the event there wasn't; only a fulsome letter of thanks which I seem to have mislaid and a not-ungenerous cash bonus. As a PS to my Lancet connection: his daughter, Francesca, expressed a desire after leaving Cambridge, to enter the advertising world. Richard and I gave her an intensive course to see her through her interview. She sailed through and we felt pride in our protégée. The fact that she was clever, funny, and beautiful may have had some bearing on the outcome. Wherever the credit lay she sailed into one of London's largest

Agencies, rose smoothly to the top and eventually retired to life in the country with two attractive children and to care for a mother who had succumbed to dementia and died a year or two ago, as had Michael, her husband. Richard and I still see 'Frannie' from time to time.

I did have about enough to live on now, but – another strange turn of fate's wheel – the bookshop was to be sold to a young genius captioned 'The Computer Kid' by the *Daily Mirror* after outstanding success on horses and dogs. This young man, David Stewart from Darlington, was evidently keen to take on an elderly person whose lifelong hobby involved horses and betting. I think that I was always a bit of an oddity to David and his young staff, Sarah senior from the North Country and Sarah junior, an Essex girl. The bookshop was soon revamped with banks of televisions round the walls and a number of computers. We had all the daily papers and we all had a hand in tipping. Sarah senior went through the card at one meeting and had a good write-up in the local paper. My persona was Professor Pink, and I had a weekly broadcast on some local radio; I never found out exactly what or where but I enjoyed it: 'This *is* Professor Pink', I fluted à la Henry Hall, the 1936 Dance Band Conductor. I also wrote a 'Weekly Comment' every week for the newsletter we sent out to the subscribers to the tips from The Computer Kid. Here are a couple of the forty-odd I wrote, just to indicate the flavour of my job.

8/2/92 – Weight and See

The Roman historian Tacitus coined a phrase '*quot homines, tot sententiae*', which translates roughly as, 'there'll be as many opinions as there are persons'. Reaction to Tuesday's publication of the Grand National weights suggest that things don't change that much!

The (apparently) lenient 12 stone which Carvill's Hill is invited to carry over 30 fences and four and a half miles (not forgetting the extra 56 yards) strikes some trainers as outrageous, others as entirely reasonable. We feel that Carvill's Hill may find the mad Aintree scramble of three dozen hyped-up equines less accommodating than, say, Chepstow's Welsh National. And will that reputedly dodgy back relish jumps, which, modified or not, are still formidable?

Moreover, only one horse has won with 12 stone. That's right: Red Rum. No wonder, as McCririck would say, 'bookies want to get Carvill's Hill'.

16/5/92 – Money 1 .... Sport 0

Call us naive but we did rather choke on our cornflakes when reading that the WTA are disappointed that their Wimbledon women's champion will get only £240,000 against the top chap's £260,000. Hardly worth the effort. Then take cricket (not including the dollar-drenched pyjama-clad variation), where four-day matches suit the marketing men, so four-day it is. And soccer's Premier League, stifled at birth by twenty-two teams where eighteen would do more for our international future.

Then there are the golfers and athletes with their rapacious 'appearance money' and the ten million pound footballers. Indeed, soccer's World Cup itself. Staged where? In the USA!

Three year old thoroughbreds are put to profitable procreation and eventually the stars endorse virtually anything that's wearable or consumable. Well, maybe you should call us naïve.

I soon realised that David was a complex character. Of course, in his chosen work he was quite brilliant. So much so, that lacking the judgement to go with it, he eventually became over-ambitious and met with disaster.

He accepted my years of involvement with horses but was also jealous. When I went to the local Ladbrokes and backed the Derby winner at 8-1, he was furious because he hadn't tipped it. I thought he was joking and didn't realise how far I'd put his nose out of joint. Although he had A-level passes, he often resented some of the words or expressions in my weekly column. Both he and Sarah senior (who also had A-levels) had no idea how to use an apostrophe. As I'm pedantic about that, it was grounds for dissension. When I raised the matter on one occasion, they told me they 'hadn't done' apostrophes. David took a fancy to some girl and it became clear that he had no idea how to deal with developing any kind of relationship. We were all convinced that he was a virgin; but didn't risk offering any advice. David had a horse called (inevitably) The Computer Kid. It was quite a good animal though not top flight. David ran it in the six-furlong Coventry Stakes at Royal Ascot. I backed it at 66-1 and was a bit hopeful after five furlongs but fourth was the best it could do.

And he was generous. On one occasion he took us and our nearest out to dinner at a local restaurant. Also present was the yearned-for girlfriend. It was only as the evening drew to a close that we realised that David was hopelessly drunk and, as the saying goes, making a public exhibition of himself. I think it terminated any chance of romantic success. As I've indicated, his undisputed cleverness was strictly one-dimensional. Thus when he came in one day and told me that his snappy little red sports car wouldn't start, questioning soon revealed that he'd never, ever realised you had to put oil in the engine. Hence it had seized up. The cost of a new engine was very large indeed. I can't remember whether he bothered, or maybe couldn't afford it.

It was probably the year after this incident that David went to the Breeders' Cup in America. He brought me back a Breeders' Cup tie, which I still wear from time to time. Things went steadily downhill and the day came when we were all out of work. I was seventy-five and had gone to work most days for forty-seven years. So there was nothing I had to do. I did rather wonder what was I *for*?

CHAPTER 12

1995-2009. CARING FOR ZENA

In due course that didn't seem to matter. The days didn't seem to take much filling. Morning tea in bed with the *Daily Telegraph*; shopping; bridge with friends; daily walk with Zena on Wimbledon Common; books to be read; supper, TV, early bed. The time passed pleasantly enough and, of course, there was always Pilots. Porthcothan remained as enchanting as ever – more, perhaps, now that over its pleasures hung the shadow of the finishing post. As we walked from Bedruthan Steps we remembered the earlier days when 'Strongers' used to wheel the quite primitive provisions up to Pilots in his wheelbarrow. Sometimes the Strongman ladies used to help: Gertrude, his wife, and his two daughters Grace and Amelia. Les Dames Strongman were possibly the three plainest ladies (well nourished on pasties) ever in one family, though they were very pleasant. Grace took over the shop when Daddy retired (or died – I can't remember which) and we got to know her quite well, and shared her sadness when her beloved Dalmatian ran off the edge of the local cliffs into the sea far below. The days of beach grounders were past for Mervyn and me though not the younger ones. We watched them, remembering the days when the ashtray on the mantelpiece had to be kept well stocked with shillings for the meter (and – something discovered years later – a useful income for Pete and Carey to plunder to re-stock sweets and Kelly's ice cream cornets). The china ducks flew up the living room wall and the 'villainous Toby Jug' squatted on the shelf in the corner. Along the cliffwalk was a seat where Zena and I used to sit watching the Atlantic rollers pound against the rocks. The boys called it *Golden Years*. One year it had been smashed up – at first we thought it must have been by the wind and the weather, but finally concluded that vandals had been at work – even here in the far west. Porthcothan was the perfect holiday destination. We were lucky, that day fifty-four years ago.

Our last stay was in 1997. I had good cause to remember it because I was struggling with my second bout of clinical depression. This had struck

Golden Wedding celebration, summer 1998.

again in the spring and was worse than my first time. Oh, I recognised all the symptoms: loss of appetite; nights spent listening to the World Service; the hopelessness which made me realise the literal meaning of despair. We used to drive up to Wimbledon Common but instead of our walk, we'd sit on a certain seat where Zena would hold my hand as I gazed bleakly into the tree-lined distance. Later, when I had recovered, we called this The Depression Seat. It was her fortitude at those times which reinforced my long-held expectation that Zena would be there on my dying day. She came from a hardy line of nonagenarians whereas with my immediate family it was 'use by date eighty'. I wasn't to know that twelve years later it would be I who sat tearfully beside her bed as she slipped slowly and peacefully away.

But back to 1997. I went to see my GP who prescribed what I recognised as Prozac, the so-called Happiness Pill. Unfortunately, I turned out to be one of those people on whom the side effects had just the opposite outcome. Appetite remained absent as did unbroken sleep. And worse, were the panic attacks. I'd heard of these but hadn't realised the unreasoning terror which sweeps over you. Of course, I shouldn't have been driving, let alone to Cornwall, but I suppose I hoped that the peace of the sky and sea might banish the misery. Accordingly I drove the 260 miles to Pilots, hands drenched with sweat as I fought for normality. I'm afraid I didn't do much for the family's holiday. Although the boys reassured me that I'd be better once the Prozac kicked in, it didn't happen and most of the time I lay on the bed, misery to myself and a burden to the others. Even the delectable Crab and Dover Sole from Padstow were flavourless and largely untouched – the most telling symptom of all!

I can't remember whether it was my own idea or whether some sensible person suggested it, but I stopped taking the ineffectual Prozac and lo! The Black Dog slunk off and has, so far, not reappeared. Just in time, too, because in 1998 we had our Golden Wedding anniversary party. We used the rooms hired out in one of the buildings at King's College where the boys had been at school. It was a great evening with lots of friends (some, alas, now departed) and we spilled out onto the terrace in the sunshine, which, as in 1948, blessed the occasion.

Later that year I had my first cataract operation at St. George's Hospital in Tooting: a locale I was to get to know all too well in the coming years. As it happened, this operation turned out (after initial success) to be something of a failure. Some years later, the lens had to be removed and replaced. The young Greek surgeon who performed this operation told me the sight would never be as good as the second eye which was done by Malcolm Thompson the No. 1 at St. George's, whom I saw privately once or twice when the first operation started going wrong. It's a truism that cataract operations do seem to the recipient a miracle. It's one of the reasons I donate to Sight Savers International who – for a mere pittance – give sight – and hope – to the poor in far-off lands.

So. My working life – or at least my working-for-money life – had ended. I was, apparently, headed for what Rupert Brooke described as, 'that serene which men call age', though that would have come many years earlier when he wrote those lines. He would probably have been brought up (like me) to regard three score years and ten as a target. Never could I have visualised being in my nineties, or even seeing in the millennium which was only a year or two away. Bearing in mind that my parents were only naturalised about 1900, they brought me up with positively Anglo-Saxon attitudes.

My father always used to regard himself as *plus royaliste que le roi* in his intense admiration of all things British, which had indeed brought him to the country of those who expelled him from what he had begun to regard as his own – South Africa.

And I remember that my mother – expecting stoic behaviour – always used to tell me, when patching up some painful childhood injury, to 'remember the wounded soldiers' – I suppose it was an echo of the First World War.

Thus I – and some contemporary friends – were appalled at the slobbering sentimentality surrounding the death and funeral of Princess Diana.

The thing I remember about the millennium is the (gloatingly reported) disastrous cock-up at the Dome when various VIPs couldn't get in; and the sight of Her Majesty, forced to link arms with the Artful Dodger and sing Auld Lang Syne. I liked to imagine the Duke of Edinburgh's comments when they were safely out of earshot later that night.

I see also from a small document dating back a quarter of a century that in 2000 I had 25 migraines – the worst total since 1986, when, for some reason, I started recording them. 166 I'd undergone by 2003 when I had more important things to worry about. Zena was also smitten by quite severe migraines; a gene we have, alas, bequeathed to Pete. Luckily, he has access to rather more and better remedies than us: a cold cloth on the forehead and lying in the dark was often the best we could manage. I vividly recall my first migraine. 1934 or '35 it would have been. I am in chapel (in the choir) singing the first verse of the hymn (409?) *When I Behold the Wondrous Cross* when I suddenly realise that I can't behold anything much for the fog that has clouded my vision. My God! Is this the dreaded blindness prophesised by the muscular Christians at the summer camp? The perils inevitably linked with 'pennis' activity? Vision does eventually return and I decide that over-indulgence in a certain brand of peppermint has been responsible. Later, of course, came red wine, dark chocolate, oranges, you name it.

Another notable migraine occasion was in 1960-something. The niece of a Canadian friend of Zena's had invited us to dinner in a block of flats near Battersea Bridge. She was rather unusually called Eliot and insisted on starting 'discussions' on things. There was a faintly *Who's Afraid of Virginia Woolf?* atmosphere about the gathering, most of which I missed because I spent the evening lying in the dark in the bedroom. Apart from the obvious embarrassment, I'd like to have spent more time talking to Mrs Cornwell, a very charming lady who turned out to be the mother of John Le Carré.

I don't think Eliot asked us over for another discussion. Mention of Eliot reminds me of another transatlantic visitor of that era: Jan Lockard, niece of one of Zena's Canadian friends and an enjoyably skilful bridge player. Her bad sportsmanship was Olympian, something embodied after her departure as 'The Jan Lockard Award' earned thereafter by whoever had behaved most unacceptably at our family bridge.

'I think this lady has vascular dementia,' began my GP's letter to the consultant at St Anthony's. Seven words in 2000 which were to define the next nine years of my life. All the other events, some of them quite significant, were overshadowed by the slow, inexorable mental decline of my once-sparkling wife. Although her condition was officially confirmed late in 2000, I had realised early in the year that something was amiss; probably due to the numerous TIAs or mini-strokes she'd suffered for several years.

We'd be on our daily walk when she'd ask me something she knew perfectly well. 'Oh yes, of course,' she'd say when I gave her the answer. There have been so many accounts of dementia in recent years; indeed the word features daily in the press and on radio and TV. But back then, I had only a very limited understanding of the condition. As I read literature from The Alzheimer's Society and *Iris*, John Bayley's account of his wife's illness, I soon realised the ordeal that lay ahead for us both.

At first, the little things: vacuum cleaning on Sunday; unable to produce coffee because she didn't know how to plug in the machine; suddenly asking, 'Jack, where is our cat?' (long since dead). And, on Tuesday mornings, I had to stand over her while she dawdled argumentatively over the glass of water she had to drink with her osteoporosis tablet. There were days when she got up at 4.30 a.m. because she 'thought you called me' or started to cook supper at 4.30 p.m. Of course, within a fairly short time she couldn't cook – and saucepans regularly ran dry and had to be thrown away. I used to get furious which was pointless, but a foretaste of that inevitable (and later, so regretted) anger, when, for example our silver apostle spoons disappeared – presumably into the dustbin. Or the house keys were hidden. As now I go on our daily walk across the common, reciting verses from *The Rubaiyat* or *The Ancient Mariner*, I remember those occasions of futile anger with great regret. So difficult at the time to see things in context, like slavery or children up chimneys. By 2001, Zena had become painfully confused at the Tesco check-out and certainly not capable of shopping on her own. I tried, with some early success, to stop her getting up too early – helped, I have to admit, by some low dosage Temazapam tablets from our GP. One day that winter she asked me at 5 p.m., 'Jack, I haven't seen our cat all day'. 'Didn't you know our cat was dead?' 'Yes, I forgot.'

TRIPS WITH THE FAMILY

With Zena at Pegasus Bridge, Normandy, 2002.

It was about then that I had to supervise her pill-taking myself to avoid usage at the wrong time or wrong day. These things sound immensely trivial now, but I can remember how furious they, and a repeated question every few minutes, used to make me. I was in contact with Social Services who used to come in for regular assessment of Zena, though I can't quite remember why. At some point it was decided that some senior psychiatric honcho would come and talk to Zena to explain why I needed occasional respite. She was a bit indignant. '*I* never get any respite', she exclaimed after they'd gone. It was always difficult to know how much Zena understood about her condition. I had explained in suitably diffused terms about the TIA damage to her brain, but it was so wonderfully typical of her old persona that her reaction on being told of the visit of the specialist was, 'They just want to check whether I'm dotty.'

In the Ardennes with Richard, 2006.

With Peter, Isle of Wight, 2010.

She referred to herself as dotty on more than one occasion, but I never truly knew how fully she understood her condition. As time passed, her habits changed completely. From reading three or four books a week, she stopped reading everything except the postcards we received from friends and family overseas. When I tried to put on an interesting radio programme, she begged me to put it off. The noise upset her. She now insisted on having a hot water bottle more or less all the year round and urged me to fill mine even though, as she knew, I used an electric blanket – and had given her one, too. By late in 2002 she began to ask whether Roie, the sister to whom she was so close, was calling, though Roie had always lived in Vancouver and in any case had been dead for some ten years. As I was putting her to bed one evening in October, she wept, 'I shall never see Roie again'. I tried, clumsily I fear, to comfort her. She asked about Roie most days till the end of her life. Once, when I was putting her to bed: 'If Roie were to come to the house you would let her in?' I explained why this was unlikely but added that, even so, if Roie did arrive I would immediately open the door. She seemed reassured, relaxed.

For the first few years of Zena's illness I kept a small notebook. As she approached her birthday that year, I told her one evening she seemed rather nervy. 'I've got plenty to be nervy about'. 'Why?' 'Someone has been pinpointing me.' 'Where?' 'When I was in the house.' 'How?' 'I don't know.' She was relieved when I suggested that she'd been imagining it. As I have said, she never dropped the subject of her sister. It was just after the above episode that at 10pm one evening my bedroom door opens, ('once again' I have noted): 'If Roie arrives later, you *will* let me know, won't you?' I promise to do so, not mentioning Roie's death. I did so a day or two before and she commented, 'Oh well, I'm a bit dotty I suppose'. I seem to have noted that this was only her second use of the word.

By this time, early 2003, she asks on most days whether Roie is coming over, adding on more than one occasion, 'I'm worried about Mother,' who has, of course been dead for three decades.

By then, I am having difficulty persuading her to bathe and put out clean clothes for her at regular intervals as otherwise she wouldn't have changed them. Could this be the woman who bathed daily, sometimes twice? One evening that January I remind her that we are expected to play bridge with some old friends. Five minutes later she comes into my room in her nightdress. No recall of our conversation.

Something happened in January that year that made me once again unsure of how aware Zena was of her condition. I mentioned that Adam, the boy next door (aged about ten) was better after being ill. 'That's good, Peter will be able to play with him.' After I explained that Peter was nearly forty-five, she seemed to see the funny side, wasn't at all upset.

Early one morning before breakfast a month later, Zena suddenly said, 'Shall we be taking our bedding with us when we leave?' 'Leave for where?' 'When we go home.' 'We live here.' 'Oh.' 'Where did you *think* home might be?' 'Vancouver?' she asked. That evening, I settled her down at 8.30pm (she always scuttled off to bed as soon as supper was over). At 9.30 she came in to my room. 'Aren't you going to say goodnight to me?' As I put these memories on paper again (from some fragmentary notes I kept for over four years after that letter from my GP) I am racked with remorse as I recall the small white-haired little lady who held so firmly on to my arm as, for twenty-five years, we trudged across the common every day it wasn't raining; stopping half way at 'Jumbo and Shane' the seat in memory of – presumably – two faithful canines. 'It's good here, isn't it?' I used to say to her. 'Lovely', she'd reply. The boys and I scattered her ashes there one cold still morning last winter. But I have jumped ahead and back then, just after my birthday, Zena woke me up (I usually slept early) to say that someone was ringing the doorbell. I went to the door, pointed out that nobody was there and explained that I sometimes thought I heard the bell but decided that it had to be the fag end of a dream. (That was actually true, but I wanted to comfort her and would have said it anyway.)

It was about this time that Social Services arrived once again, nudged by my GP who felt that I needed some respite afforded by a day at the nearby Day Centre. This was duly arranged but after they'd gone, Zena said, 'I don't want to be sent to an institution.' I explained that the Day Centre was no such thing and she agreed – grudgingly – to give it a try. A day or two later the staff collected her at 10am and she got in a bus with a number of depressed-looking old people. At 12.15 I received a phone call. Zena had walked out. A rescue mission car was sent out and located her on the Ridgway (a steep walk) and brought her home. 'I sat there for 3 hours', she told me, 'and nobody said a word to me. I didn't go into lunch', she added, 'it was pork stew'. Secretly I had some sympathy. They did look a rather miserable bunch. Needless to say the Day Centre people weren't anxious to repeat the experiment. 'We can't force people to attend', was the way the Manager put it to me.

Eventually I found a really good place. The darling District Nurse called Alice who had been looking after me for some minor infection told me about Arthur House at Wimbledon Park, only a few minutes away by car.

I went to see the Supervisor, and took to her immediately. She was kind, empathetic and helpful and said that Zena could come for a day, a week or indefinitely should the need arise. The staff – mostly young – were all warm and welcoming. 'I used to take Zena there every Friday morning. At first there were the bitter recriminations – 'I can't believe that you could leave someone here' – but before long she accepted it; only needing the assurance that I'd be back for her by four.

Zena spent a week there during one of my various operations. The boys and I got to know the staff quite well and became friends with Noreen who ran the place. It was to Arthur House that I had to move Zena when incontinence and her illness made my GP feel that I couldn't cope with her at home any longer.

But all this was in 2009. Six years earlier, things were becoming difficult to bear.

'Are we going to 12th Avenue?' asks Zena, as one morning I drive us out to the start point for our walk. She sometimes reverts to these locations of her childhood in Vancouver. Are we going to 2015, 14th Avenue West, for example; her old home. She thinks about those past days quite often. At bedtime one evening: 'Jack, it's ages since I heard from my family. Where are they all?' 'I'm afraid they've all died.' 'When?' 'Roie about twelve years ago, Heck about nine.' 'I didn't know.' 'Actually I did tell you, it must have slipped your mind.' 'The death of my brother and sister would hardly have slipped my mind', (so much for my ineptly unsuccessful tact). 'I'm the last one left.' 'Well, so am I. It's what happens when you get old.' By now she usually accepted this sort of explanation with equanimity. I put her light out at 8.30 p.m. At 9.15 she comes into my room with her shoes and socks on, carrying her clothes. Couldn't believe it wasn't morning. I said didn't she look at her bedside radio clock (it's still there) which had a clear lighted dial, but she found this confusing.

It was about this time – late 2003 – that her persistent visits – sometimes up to four – after I'd put her to bed became really difficult. I had by then a new doctor, my own having retired. This was a young woman from the north somewhere, my first lady doctor. I had misgivings but they soon vanished. She was kind, understanding and very helpful. So, for that matter, were the replacements during her several pregnancy absences. In fact, I think that I would now prefer a woman doctor. They seem to have more patience, something perhaps more appreciated by us rather slow-witted oldies. Dr J's last replacement looked about fifteen but it was she who quite strictly insisted on my going to hospital to confirm my cancer symptoms. This new young doctor a year or two later prescribed some anti-anxiety pills – Seroquel, which I later discovered were much used – some said over-used for psychotic conditions. Anyway, Zena's evening visits then more or less stopped; which was effective for *my* anxiety, too. On the subject of women doctors, I think it was the last time I was in St. George's, a place I've grown to know all too well, that a rather pretty young doctor came to my bed and said, 'I'm afraid I'm going to have to examine your back passage. Sorry, but it'll be rather unpleasant for you.' 'Well', I said (aiming to be sympathetic), 'it'll be rather unpleasant for you, too.' I think she said it went with the job. That's hospital for you; not even your arsehole's your own.

But back to November 2003. Zena's mental state had slowly but steadily deteriorated: inability to remember things for more than a few minutes; an endlessly repeated question; faulty recognition of people and sometimes weeping fits when reminded of Roie's death, with wild accusations of not being told anything. One autumn morning she came into my room and asked, 'Should I put on nice clothes today?' When I asked why, she reasoned, 'Well, it's Christmas.' Christmas ... I remember how in the early days of her illness, the joy had gone out of her (and our) Christmas – an occasion she had touched with magic in the past. I always ended the day in tears in the bathroom raging against fate or god or whatever; like Sophie in Styron's novel *Sophie's Choice*: Fuck God.

So many of her personal habits started to go into reverse. She, who had always been so fastidious, starts to leave the lavatory door open, fails to pull the plug. On one occasion I told her she must try to remember to shut it, she said, 'I did. It blew open.' This on a day in summer 2003 when there hadn't been a breath of wind. But like most of her lies it had a kind of childish transparency which makes it difficult to get angry; though it *is* undeniably aggravating.

On New Year's Eve Zena asks me at supper, 'Are we going to Richard for Christmas dinner?' Although she knows that Pete is in New Zealand, she asks several times a day whether he and Richard are coming to see us. A lot of this must sound trivial. Is trivial. Let me give you another example. One day around Easter 2004, the boys had been to lunch, so I produced a snack – toast, slice of meat, grapes – for supper. 'I can't eat any supper', she says. About 8 p.m., I tell her she can have the bathroom. 'Why should I want the bathroom?' I explain that she has a wash before she goes to bed. 'But what about supper?' I explain, and go down to the kitchen to wash up and get the breakfast things ready. She stands watching me, says if there's anything you want me to do, say. I badly want to scream out I want you to leave me alone for a minute (she hasn't for two hours). We go upstairs. Why haven't we had supper she asks, declines my offer to get her some toast and cheese. Finally goes to the bathroom and tells me (again) that she's going to bed.

I think it was during 2004 that things started getting thrown away. Most missed – and never traced – were the Apostle Teaspoons, a wedding present for my parents and hallmarked 1895. I'd buy her flowers and two days later, just when they were at their best, they'd be thrown on the rubbish heap in the garden. Sometimes I'd demand (angrily) to know why, but I gave this up because she either simply didn't know or would say, 'I can't remember'. The same fate awaited melons or tomatoes which I'd put on the living room window-sill to ripen in the afternoon sun. I usually managed to rescue them before they received the attention of passing birds or cats. Bringing some back in one day, Zena asks me, 'I want to spend a penny. Is that all right?' Why is she asking me, I say. 'Because you're there.' (Reasonable in its own quite unreasonable way.) It was from about the middle of that year that I realised that a sort of watershed had been reached beyond which it was no longer possible to ask Zena to carry out quite simple tasks. For example, one evening I was watching TV at 6.10 p.m., having prepared supper. I asked her to go down and heat the fat in the frying pan and cook the fish which was prepared. Five minutes later she comes up and asks me to come and help her. In the kitchen, the butter has burned. The fish is still in the larder. She had forgotten what to do. Again, one evening I went to a Residents' Association Committee Meeting, leaving a detailed note: my location, phone number and time of return. Do go to bed, I say, and don't wait for me to get back. But when I get back I find her downstairs and a note from Jo, our neighbour over the road, saying the phone was apparently off the hook and Zena had been standing in the window all evening. The phone had, in fact, been replaced incorrectly (as it was always from this time onwards) but Zena swore that there had been no calls and that *she* hadn't touched the phone.

One evening that summer at about 6.15 p.m. I ask her to put on the potatoes (ready in the pan) and light the oven. I go down five minutes later to get supper ready. The floor around the cooker is awash, the grill pan full of water and the area under the gas jets soaking. As – on hands and knees – I mop up the kitchen floor Zena denies all knowledge, eventually screaming out that she bloody well hadn't done it, *I* had. I began to wonder how long I could cope. I suppose it all added up to stress – something which nowadays covers everything from frontline service in Afghanistan to sitting your GCSEs. In my case, I noticed pain in my jaw when on our daily walk. I recalled that Ma had suffered from this before she had heart trouble and

At the Imperial War Museum with Peter for the D-Day 60th anniversary celebration.

reported to Dr Jo who sent me to the dreaded St. George's. I saw a most efficient Nurse Practitioner who diagnosed angina and recalled me a few days later for an angiogram which involves shooting some dye into your arteries which, when photographed, indicates where they are blocked.

As I waited to go home at the end of the day, the Ward Sister told me to forget it; they would be operating the next day: something called an angioplasty which involved sending a small balloon to open up your cardiac arteries and inserting tiny tubes to open up any blockage. As with anything serious, the NHS was first class. But as my three blocks were rather difficult to open up, the procedure took about an hour and a half instead of twenty-five minutes. The local anaesthetic wore off and had to be replenished; and I ended up sucking in oxygen in recovery and feeling rather sorry for myself. However, I was home a day or two later, back to daily walks and pain-free at that.

Little did I know that this was only the precursor of four more – far more daunting – surgical interventions to come in the next few years. I always felt

– still feel – it unfair that St. George's – to whom I owe so much (my life, in fact) should be a place which fills me with dread and distaste. I think that it's partly the overflowing clinics, blood test centres etc, with the inevitable wait long after your appointment time. And it's partly the miserable old (mostly) patients – which of course include me! Anyway, 2005 was marked only by routine checks. It was also marked on the 25 November by a most exciting landmark: the launch of my book *Field of Fire*, at the Imperial War Museum. Thanks to my great nephew Simon, a journalist on *The Times*, here I was at the IWM with numerous friends and family and a gleaming stack of 50 books – all of which were gone by the end of the day. The book sold rather well for a specialised subject and a paperback edition was published in 2007. I think Zena more or less knew what it was all about and anyway enjoyed seeing her boys, family and close friends, all of whom made a fuss of her. Apart from receiving what I considered an enormous advance, the real thrill was receiving letters from many friends and strangers to whom the book seemed to have brought much pleasure. What a thrill at eighty-seven!

The next year was not a good one. The silver lining was indeed provided by the large number of kind letters I received after the book came out. One, from a rather eminent judge (retired), reminded me how his Excellency and I had competed for MM's favours as we sailed towards Suez. But Zena – the person – was now gone. I tried to adjust – not always successfully – to watching over her full-time. I got used to deciding on her clothes each day, to helping her dress, to giving her a bath or shower. 'I'll wash you', I'd say, 'but you must wash The Vulgars.' (When Pete was a small boy entering a rather chilly Cornish sea, he'd cry out, 'it feels very cold when it hits The Vulgars!' The saying remained with us.) She became upset if I left her alone, so when I went shopping she liked to be taken along and waited quite contentedly in the car. But this sort of life engendered a gloomy atmosphere. Many mornings I awoke to feelings encapsulated by Section VII from *In Memoriam*:

> He is not here; but far away
> The noise of life begins again,
> And ghastly thro' the drizzling rain
> On the bald street breaks the blank day.

Moreover, my mornings were now visited by a ferocious attack of sciatica. I walked downstairs shouting with pain – only partly helped by painkillers. In the end, I went to see Dr M. (as my own Dr was away having one of her

Bella.

incessant babies). Dr M. always described himself as being a grumpy old bugger and generally difficult, but on the few times I'd consulted him, I'd liked and respected him. On this occasion I had to ask him if I could lie on the floor (which eased the pain). 'You need to see a neurosurgeon,' he said, and made an appointment. I took Peter to St. George's, partly for moral support and also because he is better than me at dealing with the doctors. I was given a CT scan and I'll spare you the details, but spinal surgery was the outcome and in due course I found myself back in a hospital gown and a small ward. One of my companions was visited by his fat peroxide blonde wife and a very obese son, who on arrival switched the personal TV on at full volume and sat gawping at it mindlessly while munching bags of chips. Then there was the little Spanish nurse who insisted, regardless of my denials, that I was constipated which called for a *supposeetery* to be pushed up my bottom several times. Eventually, I was taken to X-ray which confirmed that I was indeed *not* constipated, and the little nurse (reluctantly I think) abandoned my sphincter. After the operation I was cocooned and more or less helpless, but stop! What now? An overflowing bladder and only a trickle to relieve it. (Or not.) Twenty-nine years of dubious prostate had succumbed to the general anaesthetic. At 2 a.m. one morning in came a doctor and a dreaded catheter was inserted which, in the event, was not removed for another five months. I was miserable and missed my little cat Bella, for whom I wrote this poem:

Night Thoughts: A Dialogue

Oh please where has my Purrson gone?
True, there are kindly ones who give me food and affection
But when I float bedwards
To nestle in Purrson's hollow
There is no Purrson.
He's not there to receive a mouse-offering
Which he might perhaps enjoy English-style
Or maybe kosher or even (these days) halal.
There will he scratch as only he knows how
The top of my pointy head and
Speak comforting feline after-day talk
Oh missing Purrson parlez-moi d'amour...

I am here across the firmament of SW19
My little tabby formerly-homeless cat.
I too yearn for after-day purr
And the sweep of lavish whiskers
On my cheek; and the cool
Nuzzling wet nose on my neck.
Purrson is pawly at present
But soon he will return – and swiftly,
On the paws of the morning.

After a day or two, my lovely Staff Nurse S. said, 'I'm going to give you a shower.' Until then, it had been bed wash – notably by another, very young, Spanish nurse who studiously avoided my genitals as though plague-carriers. Eagerly I tottered to the bathroom on faltering twigs and sat on the chair. Oh what bliss the warm water and oh, how splendidly did Staff Nurse S. cleanse my unwholesome body! Can there be a less appetising sight than a constipated old man with a catheter stuck in his penis? When Richard collected me some time later and drove me to my niece Monica (in Amersham) to recuperate, I was in an optimistic mood: all too soon to prove misplaced. I'd only been there a few days, enjoying her luxurious cooking, when one evening I collapsed and only with great difficulty arose from the floor like some wounded camel. Poor family. Monica, convinced, not unreasonably, that I was about to die, summoned an emergency doctor (who talked of anaemia) and Richard, who hired a private ambulance at fearful cost, to take me – you guessed – back once again to St. George's; this time to A&E where I had suffered a bleed they told me; my haemoglobin had dropped to a really alarming 4 point something. Six units of blood were dripped into me with an eminent consultant and acolytes watching as the rush of blood to my-none-too-sturdy heart gave me a really frightening angina attack – watched by the unfortunate Pete who was visiting. Up to some faraway operating theatre I was whisked and late one evening underwent (sedated but struggling) an exceedingly painful op via my throat, to treat a duodenal ulcer. Poor Richard saw me wheeled back to the ward looking, he told me later, the colour of skimmed milk. However, the NHS had once again succeeded when most needed and the ulcer, discouraged by the Omeprazole I take each day, has remained quiescent. (At one point I was on fourteen pills a day, but this has now reduced to eight.)

Poor Zena during this time had to go to an NHS Care Home in distant Norbury. She hated it but was remarkably stoical. Richard and Peter were wonderfully helpful and went there frequently to take her out for lunch and a walk. I phoned her as often as I could to assure her that we'd soon be reunited at home. And back at home, some helpful things were happening. Richard had discovered an Agency who sent me Maria, the Greek Treasure (and her omni-skilled husband George). Just as I was wondering one day some weeks later how long I could afford the Agency fees, she exclaimed, 'Why you pay all that money to Agency? I can work for you privately.' To which she added that her fee would be half what I paid the Agency. Indeed, it was far too little and in due course – dismissing her protests – I increased it, though not as much as I wanted – and she refused. Maria doesn't just do my evening meal six days a week, but irons my clothes (the best shirt ironer in my life except for Zena), washes the floor, deals with the dustbins and has worked out where everything goes to the last teaspoon. She also cooks me Greek delicacies like stuffed vine leaves, having heard stories of my eleven trips to her homeland. The downside is her annual two-monthly visit to her house in Lemnos; but even here she has briefed and supplied me with two excellent replacements. A real joy is to listen to one of Maria's mangled anecdotes such as the visit of her nephew to the fish and chip shop. George was elected by her to drive me to St. George's for my next op at about 6am. 'Don't worry, he will like it', she assured me.

My next op; yes. As I've explained I now went through life attached to a catheter. In January 2007 I was summoned to a TWOC (Trial Without Catheter) at the Place of Doom. Encouraged by Pete, I drank jug after litre jug of water, but my obstinate innards would not allow me to produce more than a few drops as I stood bloated and cursing over the loo. Bursting with frustration and urine, I had the catheter once again inserted. I could pee but I was afraid of the TURP operation which was now inevitable. As I've described, the beautiful Indian doctor spent what seemed to be a very long time as I watched the clock and tried – without success – to remember how long. On this occasion they had inserted a catheter which seemed about the diameter of a stick of macaroni (to clear the debris apparently) and I realised that its removal would involve an ordeal to come. The morning came for this to be done and my morale was not lifted when the patient in the next bed underwent the same procedure to the accompaniment of yelps and screams. It wasn't as bad as I'd expected. (It couldn't have been.) This time it was Richard's turn to take me to the Clinic where the sister absolutely guaranteed that I would pee again. I waited there. I waited and waited there. Willy at the ready. Yes! a modest, but undeniable (and increasing) flow emerged from my battered member. Back quickly, then, to Richard with a thumbs up. We were (almost) equally thrilled.

Another *very* helpful thing: I was able to take respite every Thursday afternoon because my kind neighbour Jo-over-the-road had Zena for the afternoon, including tea. (Her title is to distinguish her from Jo-next-door a close friend, much loved by Zena and all of us, who arrived thirty-one years ago. She and Nigel her husband (our dentist) and their children have shared so many memories with us. She still signs cards and phone calls as Jo-next-door though she lives a little way off in Wimbledon Village.)

Jo-over-the-road is a relative newcomer after a mere seventeen years, but has become a true friend especially after Maurice, her husband, died on Christmas Day 1999. As one holding all our mobile numbers, as well as our house keys, she is always the unfortunate first point of call whenever anything goes wrong – like when I fell into the bus, broke my nose, bled like a pig and was carried off in an ambulance. She feeds my little cat Bella if I'm not around. Zena was always comfortable with Jo and loved her Thursdays with her, though she became anxious about my reappearance by four o'clock. 'Thank you for having me,' she'd say to Jo as we left. One of those freakish aspects of Zena's condition was, Jo told me, that, watching

Countdown, she'd occasionally get an eight letter word, an echo, perhaps, of the years when we did the *Telegraph* crossword together.

It is late June and what I call the Annual Martyrdom, when normal life in Wimbledon is sacrificed to the demands of The Centre Court etc. This is one of the few things about which Zena and I used to disagree. She enjoyed tennis and used to go to the Centre Court, notably in our early days when she was given a ticket by an elderly lady called Grace Dewey. Mrs Dewey, a Debenture holder whatever that was, used to play when the Tournament was held in Worple Road; and I think Zena told me that she'd been the first – or one of the first – women (or 'ladies' at Wimbledon) to serve over-arm. Anyway by 2008, Zena still seemed to enjoy – or at least to tolerate – the tennis on the TV I'd installed in her bedroom. She wouldn't watch or listen to anything else. 'It's so noisy', she'd say. I used to call the tennis 'biff' short for biffbat and, although I admire the stamina and technique of some players, I find the rampant egoism intolerable.

The players who achieved fame through appallingly bad behaviour (eg Nastase, McEnroe) ruined the game for me. As for what they called 'grunting' – apparently by the ladies but it seemed far more like the sound of mating foxes – I would have had those players (Seles, Sharapova) simply given a warning and then disqualified. I once met most of the American Team playing in the tournament at Gazeira in Cairo. Here were some of the world's top players (I drop no names) with maybe eight brain cells between them. Then again I find the mildly hysterical tennis audience what I can only call silly. Add to all that the far-flung road closures and universal 'No Parking' and you can see why I 'go Meldrew', (as a reactor goes critical) during this stressful fortnight. I wonder how many people still remember the furore over Gussie Moran's knickers or dear old Teddy Tinling and the 'my word!' and 'ooh I say!' chap who did the commentary. Not sure I remember his name: Dan Maskell? But in the summer of 2008, I had more than biff to add to an already stressful life.

There was the always alarming sight of blood in my pee. I went to see the apparent schoolgirl who was standing in for the ever-pregnant Dr. Jo. She turned out to be quite grown-up and severe and insisted on making an appointment for me at St. Doomladen. The doctor at the Day Surgery managed to find and anaesthetise my terrified and shrunken willy and eventually withdrew the little camera and announced that I had a tumour in my bladder. I asked – rather dimly – what next? He said he would cut it out. A few days later I discovered that my niece Ann Louise had had this same operation seven years before; but being more courageous than her ancient uncle, had not thought to mention the matter. From her, I found out rather more than I wanted to know about cancer of the bladder, incontinence etc, and arrived early one morning in the New Year at St. G's (piloted by Maria's ever-willing husband George) in the usual apprehensive frame of mind. The routine de-humanising process: questions, identity band on wrist, removal of clothes, arrival at ward filled with equally resentful strangers; though this time there seemed rather more team spirit as we all had cancer of a sort; I being lucky with a fairly forgiving type. A rather nice anaesthetist, after some discussion, told me she was going to use a local – an epidural. I was quite pleased as the last general had more or less wrecked me. I think it was a bit later that day that I found myself in the room before the theatre. The nice anaesthetist appeared. 'Here I am in all my glory,' she announced. A doctor asked me if I knew what they were about to do. 'Remove a tumour from my bladder, I hope', I replied. (Always difficult to be urbane or witty without one's teeth.)

The operation dragged on for quite a while with rushing water somewhere. As I was quite dead from the waist down I felt nothing except, at one point, as though something heavy had been dropped on to my stomach. I do remember thinking how awful it must be to become paralysed after an accident. I had this irrational wish to move my legs but of course the body wouldn't react to my mind's desire. It's an unpleasant experience.

All I can remember about that stay is the quite tasty soup at suppertime (Richard brought me in smoked salmon and other delicacies) and the enormous Turk whose snoring in the opposite bed made sleep impossible. When I asked the night nurse to move him or something she quite indignantly told me that this would be infringing his human rights. 'But what about *my* right to try to sleep?' I queried. It seemed it didn't exist. I was even more glad than usual to get home. Zena was in Arthur House and – guiltily – I left her there for and an additional two or three days' respite for myself.

After Zena came home, life seemed to settle in to what had become a cheerless routine. My memory of her at this time is of an unhappy face, and though she was reasonably accepting of her situation, she got little pleasure out of life. She enjoyed having Bella the cat on her lap and our daily walk. When we reached 'Jumbo and Shane', our favourite seat, we'd have a bit of a rest and I'd give her a Lifesaver fruit drop which Richard (and his friend James) used to bring from USA as they weren't obtainable in Britain. Occasionally over the years Zena would ask if we could stop for a few moments as she was out of breath. She always recovered quickly but it was a bad sign of things to come. Before long, however, something happened which changed the outlook. Night time. I am in a deep sleep when suddenly I hear someone clumping upstairs. There is a loud cry: 'Police!' and a strong light is shone on my face. 'Are you Jack?' asks the copper. I'm just about sure I am. When I go downstairs, I see Zena in her nightgown by the front door. She'd been wandering down the main road towards Wimbledon when – presumably – a police patrol had seen her. 'You'd better watch your front door,' advised the cop; and, indeed, from that day onwards, I locked the mortice every night – keeping the key safely with me. I didn't ask Zena what she was doing because I knew she couldn't have told me. What she did (surprisingly) say was, 'People must feel sorry for you, having a wife that's mad.' This was another occasion on which I wondered exactly how aware she was of the bad thing that had happened to us.

For many months I had more or less refused to consider moving Zena into a home, even though close friends told me that it was reaching a point where it would be her or me. By the middle of the year, Zena was becoming incontinent. Dr Jo, on finding that I was having to wash Zena's soiled clothes and generally beginning to buckle under the strain, told me that the time had come for her to leave home.

So one day late in June I took her to Arthur House. Fortunately she knew the place and the staff who were always so good to her. She had a pleasant little room. There was Sophie the black and white cat and people qualified to take care of her. I don't believe I could have left her in a strange place. As it was, I was racked with guilt taking her from home and everything so familiar. We told her it was just for a few weeks till I was fully fit again but I don't know whether she believed us.

One or other of us visited her every day – often twice. Old friends such as Carey and both the Jos spent time with her so that she didn't feel too cut off from her world. The boys and I used to take her for morning coffee. I used to walk with her to nearby Wimbledon Park. We'd pass the tennis courts and the playground with its swings and obstacles till we reached the café in the park. We'd sit on the balcony at an outside table among the young mothers and their offspring. I'd buy Zena a cappuccino as she loved spooning off the froth. I usually brought along a Kit Kat and she'd eat that. Sometimes she'd hold my hand as we sat together on a shady seat watching the children. Her face always seemed sad.

A few weeks passed, and the days seemed uneventful when one Saturday afternoon I had a call from Arthur House: Zena had 'had a turn' and been sent by ambulance to St. George's. I phoned the boys and early one evening we all met at the A&E in that place we'd grown to know all too well.

There's always something a bit intimidating about A&E: the sharp lights, the numerous medics and their machinery; and the palpably anxious ambience. After all, E does stand for emergency. So when the three of us were allowed into the treatment area, we found Zena in the first bay, recumbent and fitted with an oxygen mask. 'Come with me, guys,' ordered a capable-seeming lady doctor. In a side room she explained that Zena's problem was respiratory failure. This doctor was brisk but sympathetic. She visited us in the ward the next day – Sunday. We were all impressed. However, she made it clear that there was limited scope for putting things right. (Thinking about it afterwards, I believe that she must have thought it at least probable that this was a one-way ticket; even that Zena would not last the night.) She was to be given oxygen with a view to getting her lungs functioning well on their own. She would be moved into a ward later that evening. Thus began our anxious monitoring of her oxygen SAT levels.

Hopes rose and were dashed. Once or twice the reading was over 90, but sometimes – more often – as low as 70. We bought her favourite tasty foods from the M&S shop in the hospital: prawn sandwiches and toffee muffin dessert; though she found it difficult to eat. She was in a small ward with five other ladies – two of whom died. We got to know them all. Richard seemed to empathise most and was privy to their illnesses and prognoses. We set up a shift system so that one of us was with Zena more or less all day. We mostly fed her ourselves for the nurses simply didn't have time. I remember helping her drink from the straw which came with the little carton of apple juice. All this time she was on oxygen – either through a mask or into her nose. I think these things distressed her, but they seemed to be her best – her only – chance of survival. One morning the lady consultant called me aside and told me, albeit not in so many words, that they couldn't do any more for Zena except to, 'make her comfortable'. I was unable to hold back the tears and was comforted by the big, warm-hearted West Indian nurse. 'It's hard, man', he said, patting my shoulder. A day or two later I came in to discover that Zena was alone in a side ward. Richard, who has a knack of finding things out, told me that she had been put on the Liverpool Pathway Care. I knew that this meant that time was running out. Occasionally Zena opened her eyes but she didn't seem to see anything. She lay more or less sleeping, her breathing shallow. I spent the afternoon of 13 July sitting by her bed and talking to her in a choking voice. The hand I held was thin, quite warm but not responsive. Next morning Richard came to see me. Pete had replaced him at the hospital he said, and told the nurses that although he was no expert, Zena appeared to have died. What an ordeal for him. And for Richard. For my part, I knew that this moment would have to come; and I think I knew that I was saying my own goodbye the previous afternoon. My overwhelming sadness was for myself, not for Zena, whose long life had become a burden – now ended by peaceful death.

She and I had discussed our respective funerals from time to time, so I had a general idea: not too religious which would be inappropriate; not anti-religious which could be hurtful. As Richard said, introducing the service (at Putney Vale Crematorium) it was a sad, but not a tragic occasion. We had the Revd Millie – a nice woman Vicar (which we thought Zena would like), a favourite hymn, the 23rd Psalm, some Shakespeare from Pete and a reading from Ecclesiastes: 'Remember now thy creator in the days of thy youth ...'. Carey read from some of Zena's letters she'd written home about life in battered London after the war and our meeting. They were so like her – funny, observant and self-aware. Carey caught their mood so precisely that it was (as I told her) almost like hearing Zena herself though with an English accent. I spoke on 'Remembering Zena'. Fifty-two friends and family were there on that morning of sunshine and showers. Among them – over from Canada – was Ann Carina whose parents, lifelong friends, lived next door when she was born. A couple of years older than Richard, she was (and has remained) a surrogate sister to our boys. Coincidentally, marriage had taken her to Vancouver, living in a street near to Zena's childhood home.

Afterwards, we invited everyone to King's College School where we had celebrated our Golden Wedding eleven years before. Pete and his partner had set up some large panels containing photographs from every part of Zena's life. In most of them she was smiling or laughing; such a contrast with the small forlorn figure of those final years. So, late that evening I sat contemplating an unexpected future on my own. (Zena had come from a long-lived family whereas in mine none had exceeded eighty and most, of course, had no chance of reaching even that.) I remember that Caitlin Thomas, Dylan's widow, had entitled her memoirs *Leftover Life to Live* but that felt a bit negative. I would read some books, observe the zeitgeist, try to get another letter into the *Daily Telegraph* (no success so far) and morph into a grumpy(ier) old man. Oh, and write another book. Didn't sound too boring a programme for my nineties.

CHAPTER 13

BEING NINETY-SOMETHING

But hey! What's with the broody introspection? Have you forgotten that next month you're already booked to talk to two groups of young officers at the School of Artillery at Larkhill? This is, in fact, my fourth such talk and it came about in a rather unexpected way. After *Field of Fire* was published I was asked to give one of the Lunchtime Lectures held at the National Army Museum in Chelsea. Afterwards a pleasant ex-Royal Artillery Colonel came up, made some flattering comments and suggested that we keep in touch. And in due course, he and two fellow Colonels asked me and Bill French to lunch in Wimbledon.

The next year we invited them and it has become an annual date. These were retired officers – much younger than us – who had served in places like Korea and Northern Ireland. Bill French? My old Battery Commander, and my oldest friend (1945) with whom I now meet every week; reunited years ago by a strange coincidence. Zena and friends used to play bridge at one another's houses every week. One of the bridge fours was called Nora French. Serving the ladies with tea, I never made the connection until I met Bill in the doctors' surgery one evening and it all came tumbling out. Nora, Bill's second wife – Molly, his first wife had died soon after the war – sadly contracted cancer. I used to go and see her; and left her a Peace Rose from the garden the day before she died. Bill, an excellent bridge player (as I remembered from our post-war days in Germany) used to make up a four with us from time to time. It so happened that one of the Colonels had a connection at Larkhill, and in October 2008 invited Bill and I to the open day on which the Young Officers Group demonstrated their various gunnery skills. Before lunch we were introduced to a ridiculously youthful officer who I thought was a captain; they wear those little hard-to-see tabs hung on the front tunic button. But no, it was a crown and two pips and this was the Commandant. 'Jack Swaab?' he said, shaking my hand. 'I've

With Bill French, Larkhill, 2008.

read your book. I'd like you to talk to our Young Officers Group. Could you arrange that Paul?' he asked, turning to the Major (Paul Jones) who runs the courses.

Thus in May 2009 Peter drove me and Mervyn – resplendent in RAF tie – down to Larkhill for talk and lunch. I enjoyed giving the talk which we interspersed with readings (by Pete) from *Field of Fire*, and the noisy Chester Wilmot tape recording I describe in an earlier chapter. The YOs also seemed to enjoy the talk – amazed perhaps to hear ancient first hand tales of derring-do.

It is proper summer – sun and everything – and, sitting at Jumbo and Shane, our special seat on Wimbledon Common, I happened to look down at my arms. I was wearing a short sleeved cotton shirt and there they were: rather skinny and wrinkled (runkle in Swaabese); and I thought how unattractive compared with the smooth young arms that summer brings out with, 'the girls in their summer dresses', as described by Irwin Shaw in a short story I read decades ago.

It added to the melancholy I find it hard to resist these days. Presumably the prevailing mood of most very old people who, 'Turn the wheel and look to windward', and 'consider Phlebas, who was once handsome and tall as you.'

I had to check that I had quoted these lines correctly in my battered first edition of Eliot's *Collected Poems 1909-1935*. This book accompanied me for most of the war. Indeed, written in pencil on the flyleaf is: 'To the memory of many nostalgic moments ashore and afloat and laughs just one or two. George Long Nov 1942.' I have written about George earlier in this book. I used to know large sections of Eliot by heart; particularly 'The Love Song of J. Alfred Prufrock' which I regard as one of the great poems of our time.

To counter the weltschmerz I play bridge every few weeks. I've known the others – and played with them – for years. I'm an adequate player: 'One that will do to swell a progress, start a scene or two.' Last time I had one of those gratifying days, notably making a tight three no trump on the last card – seven of clubs. It reminded me of the first time we played at the Dobsons. Richard was a commanding sort of figure and I think we were both a bit nervous. The first hand of the day: I am looking at a mass of Royal Faces and Aces. Zena opens One Heart. There was nothing else for it ... Six Hearts I respond. Zena went quite pale but, clever player that she was, made it comfortably. 'What's the old bugger up to now?' enquired our host a few hands later. It was a jolly afternoon.

We used to stay at Mervyn's delightful villa in The Algarve where one of the unfailing events was the arrival of the numerous stray dogs on the lookout for something tasty. Chief among these was a rather charming animal whose persuasive skill led us to call him The Ingratiator. What put this in my mind was the appearance on TV of one of the lady weather forecasters whose sugary mannerisms led her to inherit the title. The forecasters have their own particular characteristics. There is Doctor Strangelove with the waving arms and wild eyes; and – immortalised by inefficiency – the ignoble Fish. You'd think – correctly – that in today's world I would not allow the nuances of weather forecasting (or even forecassting) to irritate me. But you'd be wrong. I don't know, but there has been something insidious about the way that our meaningful, robust Fahrenheit temperatures seem to have been overtaken by the uninspired Centigrade or snooty Celsius, where even very hot weather only reaches thirty something instead of that sweaty red ninety plus. And even centigrade was taken over in a rather superior way which hinted of arcane climatology known only to the weather people and flung rather snootily before us proles. There they all are, infected by weather talk: 'spits and spots' of rain, 'misty and murky' days and above all, 'low teens' as though we're discussing degenerate young people. Nobody seems able to tell me whether this Celsius-ridden situation is legal or maybe inflicted on us by the EU. And winter precipitation now comes only in millimetres or centimetres except when one of the experts forgets himself and remarks on 'a couple of feet of snow'. Luckily, the good old *Daily Telegraph* still keeps the Fahrenheit flag flying like George Orwell's aspidistra. I mean – how did all this happen? Were we ever consulted?

On *The Daily Politics* last week, a Foreign Office Minister didn't know the capital of Honduras. (Hadn't been there, he said.) I thought: I would have known that at twelve because my father often used to ask at meals the capitals of all the obscure places like Outer Mongolia, Lithuania and Honduras. It was a habit I continued with my sons – usually for some trifling money reward. One of Pete's school reports aged eleven showed him in first place in Geography with 100%. His grandfather would have been thrilled! And they, in turn, rebounded on me: Richard usually with political questions or details of cricket statistics or pop group songs and Pete with literary quotations. Only last week he asked Richard and me – for 5p – who wrote, 'What cat's averse to fish?' We didn't know.

And a year or two ago I stumped them both with, 'Who was The Man from Abilene?' I realise that ours has been a rewarding family tradition obviously not widely shared. When I watch quiz shows, the eyes of most contestants start to glaze over after the words, 'who wrote ....?'

Looking back, I realise that we were lucky; learning was a challenge and fun.

On Sundays I sometimes listen to religious services of different kinds: shouting angrily at what I regard as the credulity and absurdity of much of what I hear. Don't get me wrong; I wouldn't try to abolish the dear old C of E – ever more tolerant, woolly and indecisive, but with church music and hymns I never fail to enjoy. And what a pleasant contrast to the excesses and demands of Allah with Islam's decapitations and hostility towards everyone else. That said, I still find the basics of Christianity quite unacceptable. I mean, if we had turned the other cheek to Hitler's helpers, we would have ended with a Nazi world wouldn't we? Would Jesus have wanted that? The preacher I heard a week or two ago was thrilled that in recent times the number of Christians in Africa had multiplied by thousands of times; and by 2030 or some such date would outnumber those in the West. To me, this simply underlines how the uneducated and credulous people come to outnumber the more thinking, educated and consequently secularised populations. I remember how at school (chapel twice daily) my lips were clamped firmly shut during the recital of the Creed; something I shared with 'Kags' Lane the Science Master.

I've nothing much against Jesus though he doesn't seem to have been much fun. But I *know* that you can't feed 5,000 people with a few loaves and one or two fish. When I challenge Christian friends about this, and other miracles, they never seem quite sure whether those events are to be taken literally or as some sort of metaphor.

You'll realise, therefore, from my going into these details that nothing could make me believe in the resurrection – either of Jesus or indeed of those who followed him over the centuries. 'Resurrection of the body' – what, for the thousands vaporised in a few seconds at Hiroshima or the gas ovens of Auschwitz? I have   with some sadness – to conclude that when Jesus cried out on the cross, 'My God, my God why have you forsaken me?' it was in that moment that he realised the falsity of the words he had preached during his short life. I sympathise with the despair which finally overtook him. Of course, most of what I've written refers to the one religion about which I know at least something. But it does seem that organised religion has been responsible for most of the conflict which has characterised mankind. Think how early man, subject to the anger of the Gods, would have regarded thunderstorms. And what do today's Catholics in Haiti and Japan feel about God's mercy with its tsunamis and earthquakes?

Well, I suppose that in the end it boils down to personal faith, but this seems to entail suspension of what one sees daily; and acceptance of – for example – suffering as in some way related to the will of a merciful and loving yet contradictory deity. Doesn't make sense really, does it?

There's a picture in today's paper of the Royal Family coming ashore after a rain-swept Scottish cruise holiday. Can't have been high spot of the year from their glum expressions; seven of them and not a smile to be seen. What really struck me though was how wonderfully well the men's jackets fitted them. Even Edward's. Took me back to the fifties, when I, too, had suits that fitted. Because they were made for me. Don't get the idea that I had money. No, the suits owed their existence to the know-how of one John Standen, an Agency Account Executive, who had located some tailors in Commercial Street, E1 where a number of us from Foote Cone & Belding lost no time in getting elegantly clothed. The premises were faintly Dickensian – naked lights, steaming irons and a fitting room which comprise of one old army blanket hung up by both ends. Joe and 'Bomber' (I never found out his actual name) did the tailoring which was wonderful – several fittings – at some amazingly low price (multiplied many times over for the identical items in Joe's West End showroom). Joe's suits lasted me for years, finally defeated by old age and increasing waist measurement. I fondly remember the last one, a Prince of

Wales overcheck in grey and blue, which I finally had to take to Oxfam (bread on the waters ...) because I couldn't do the trousers up. I say bread on the waters because in the last year or two I have needed a suit for (increasingly) funerals and the occasional formal occasion such as a wedding anniversary. Reluctant to buy off the shelf and unable to contemplate made to measure, I entered Oxfam where some extremely helpful ladies (shades of Zena's years there) went to endless trouble and found me quite an acceptable suit for £25. It needed a bit of local alteration which added about £60 but I was told by the alterers that this suit – a Burberry – retailed for about £400.

But what of John Standen, the onlie begetter of our good fortune? John, along with myself and several other mates at FCB, was a regular punter on the horses. He also was a considerable – and successful – womaniser. He didn't always treat his conquests with consideration, so the rest of us were lacking in sympathy when in 1956 he became besotted with a babesome creature whose name I have forgotten, who, in that clever way that some women have, positively tortured John with (we all assumed) an occasional *hors d'oeuvre* but only the promise of a possible toothsome main course on some future occasion. John wooed her excessively – and expensively – and thus it came about that we were together listening on the radio – no TV then – to the St Leger that autumn; a race that was to provide the funds for some enormous treat designed to overcome any of the beloved's resistance. John had backed a horse called Hornbeam which had been fourth in the Derby. Fourth in the Derby, First in the Leger went the old racing axiom, and John had plunged (too) heavily on Hornbeam with a promise of (I think I remember) £750 it if won; a lot of moolah in those days.

The last two furlongs ..... Hornbeam surges to the front. All seems well when – in the last 75 yards was it? – a vile French horse called Cambremer looms alongside and, as the commentator shrieks with excitement, gets up to win. Wherever I hear or read the expression a broken man, I think of poor John that September afternoon fifty-five years ago. He recovered and married a lovely woman called Brenda. From time to time he'd phone Mervyn and say we must all meet for lunch. It never happened – probably never was going to – but John got cancer and died in 2007.

I've been (particularly) angry today. An NHS big wig called Professor Bean, is quoted as explaining how hospital beds are going to become more scarce for all because they're so heavily used by older members of the population. It so happens that Patrick, an old friend and neighbour, has been in just that situation for the last few weeks. No doubt flying his Lancaster bomber (and getting a DFC) on numerous missions when not long out of the school room didn't improve his life expectancy. Last time I visited him, there were six toothless old men in various stages of disconnection; and I thought of Mr Bean. Felt like sending him a note to apologise – though we'd served our country in desert, mud and snow – for monopolising hospital beds. We'll die as soon as we can, Mr Bean. Free up a bit of bed space.

Patrick died peacefully on the first day of 2011 at a care home around the corner. I went to see him a couple of days before. Gaunt, he emerged briefly from sleep. Long enough to say goodbye. There were air force medal wearers at his funeral, and red, white and blue flowers.

One of the plays my father took me to see was *The Insect Play* by the Capek brothers, which likened man's activities to theirs; and the grandly uniformed ant generals fought a war, 'for the land between two blades of grass'.

It has formed a background to my struggle (unsuccessful) to comprehend the concept of Creation. As an – admittedly agnostic – atheist it has been man-made God which I've found unacceptable. Expressed by Herbert Read in a wartime poem, 'God's existence: a concept beyond the mind's reach'. Though each religion will insist that it is peaceful, compassionate and loving, the facts inform one otherwise. So many of man's bloodiest episodes have been – and still are – religion-based.

I have concluded – reluctantly – that man is (although there are plenty of good exceptions) basically a bad animal, essentially selfish, acquisitive and as a result, aggressive and violent. The author Cormac McCarthy seems to agree. In *The Road*, perhaps the most frightening book I've read, he pictures a foodless USA, in which, after some unidentified disaster, the few survivors turn to murder and cannibalism.

I read, daily, warnings of future global warming, flooding, freezing. How much help will they be then, your Bible, your Koran, your Torah? Will your elderly philosophers and priests protect you? No, I fear (as an old, weak man) that the ignorant, but young, strong males will rule, brutally if necessary.

A gloomy outlook indeed. Meanwhile the weather becomes warmer, there are hints of the first green of the spring and the Ides of March approaches once again. 'I, myself near the end of the road', I wrote seven years ago. Now that end is nearer and, as I look back on what I've described in my first paragraph as my odd life, I am grateful. For my survival in war and hospital. For the women in my life; and for my friends (often the same). Most of all for my caring sons who have encouraged me in so much. *Carpe Diem!*

Wimbledon, March 2012